MARTIN LUTHER

MARTIN LUTHER

BY HARRY EMERSON FOSDICK

Illustrated by STEELE SAVAGE

RANDOM HOUSE · NEW YORK

Fourth Printing

CONTENTS

CONTENTS

9

MARTIN LUTHER

1

A Poor Boy
Who Changed
the World

ONE of the most famous days in history was April 17, 1521. On that day Charles V, sovereign of a large part of Europe, sat in state at Worms, in Germany, surrounded by leading princes, nobles, distinguished churchmen and ambassadors from foreign lands. Before them stood a solitary monk, named Martin Luther, on trial for his life. The Pope in Rome had excommunicated him, accusing him of writing books which taught false doctrine, and there on a table the books were piled.

The Emperor was demanding that Luther confess himself wrong and retract his teaching—or else! In those days the punishment for heresy—that is, for teaching anything the Roman Church thought wrong—was to be burned at the stake, and the monk knew that well. Nevertheless, he faced that brilliant, powerful assembly and said, "I cannot and will not retract anything, for it is neither safe nor right to act against one's conscience."

That occasion was one of the turning points in the story of the Western world, involving momentous consequences. Today there are more than two hundred million Protestant Christians in the world, and they all owe an unpayable debt to that monk at Worms. Far beyond Protestantism, however, the ideas and institutions of our Western world have been deeply influenced by the resolute stand of that brave man, and all of us have been affected by it.

When Martin Luther was born—on November 10, 1483—no one could have guessed that he would play so important a part in history. He came from a poor family of farmers. "I am a peasant's son," he said once. "My father, my grandfather and my great-grandfather were genuine peasants." The family lived in Saxony, in eastern Germany. At least up to the First World War there were still Luthers living in the little village of Möhre on the western side of the Thuringian hills, and from there Hans Luther, Martin's father, moved some eighty miles to Eisleben and became a miner. There Martin was born; but six months later the family moved again to the neighboring town of Mansfield, more in the center of the copper-mining district, and Martin's earliest memories are centered there.

He remembered his mother carrying heavy loads of fagots from the neighboring forest for the household's fires, and recalled her sigh of relief when the burden slipped from her shoulders to the ground. "My parents were very poor"—so he remembered. "They endured the hardest labor for our sakes." Luther's father, however, was an able man. Before many years he was leasing mines and smelting-furnaces to operate for himself and, when Martin was

7

eight years old, was elected to the Town Council where he served for the rest of his life. Martin always took pride in this early struggle of his family against poverty. He even said that he thought the children of poor families had a better chance than the children of rich families, because rich children were tempted to be proud and conceited, while poor children "must labor to lift themselves out of the dust."

Looked at from our standpoint now, those were rough days for children, whether rich or poor. Whipping was standard practice in home and school and, if Martin's remarks in later life are correctly reported, he never altogether got over feeling hurt at some of the punishments inflicted on him: "My mother caned me for stealing a hazelnut, until the blood came"; "My father once whipped me so that I ran away and felt ugly toward him until he was at pains to win me back"; "I was caned [at school] in a single morning fifteen times for nothing at all. I was required to decline and conjugate and hadn't learned my lesson."

Nevertheless, while Martin was a sensitive lad and

took this common practice of whipping with long-remembered resentfulness, he knew that he was getting what all the other boys and girls of that time were suffering too. Even of his mother's thrashing about a trifle he acknowledged that she meant it well, and he was steadfast in his devotion to his father all his life. He had a good home, stern in discipline, but full of love and loyalty. That was proved by the way his parents saw in Martin unusual possibilities, and backed him to the limit in getting an education such as no Luther had ever had before.

Martin's family was earnestly religious, and in Saxony in those days that meant being devoutly Roman Catholic. There was no other kind of Christian church and, alike in home and school, Martin was taught the Roman Catholic faith. To be sure, his father was an independent person and did not like being ordered around even by a priest. Once when Hans Luther was very sick and a priest, taking advantage of his fear of death, tried to persuade him to give money to the Church and so make his peace with God, Hans answered, "I have many children.

9

I will leave my property to them; they need it more."
Nevertheless, all the Luthers were loyal Catholics and
Martin early learned by heart the Lord's Prayer, the
Ten Commandments and the Creed, sang the psalms
and hymns, took part in the celebration of holy days,
attended Masses and vespers, and prayed to the saints,
especially Saint Anne, protectress of the miners. Every
town in Saxony was full of churches and monasteries, priests, monks and nuns, collections of sacred
relics, and shrines to which the sick came to be cured.
All these outward expressions of religion Martin took
for granted; they were part and parcel of his daily
life, and at the heart of them, especially in his home,
there was a genuine and often joyous Christian spirit.
In particular Martin loved to sing. He always reveled
in music and, as a boy, had a charming voice. His
enjoyment of singing ranged all the way from the
German folk songs at Christmas time to the stately
Magnificat in the church choir. Doubtless from that
early experience comes the fact that we still sing a
Christian hymn for children which he later wrote:

Away in a manger,
no crib for a bed,
The little Lord Jesus
laid down his sweet head.

Nevertheless, there was another side to Martin's youthful religion which one must know about if one is to understand what happened to him later. He was afraid of God. He had a very sensitive conscience; he felt miserably guilty over even small mistakes; and he heard so much about the wrath of God against sinners that he was frightened. In those days hell was dreadfully real in the imagination of all the people— a place of eternal torture to which sinners were sent when they died. And next to hell in horror was purgatory—a place where souls not good enough for heaven nor bad enough for hell were sent until by their punishments their sins were purged away. This might take thousands of years. The religion of Luther's day relied a good deal on the fear of hell and purgatory to scare people into doing right, and

Martin's sensitive conscience was terrified. He was afraid even of Christ, Who was coming as a stern judge to damn the guilty. And he later recalled how he shivered when at church in Mansfield he looked at the stained-glass window where Jesus was portrayed, with a frowning face, seated on a rainbow, on one side a lily to symbolize His blessing on the good but, on the other, a flaming sword to represent His anger against the wicked.

In his later life Martin linked up this fear of God and Christ with his fear of the stern punishments he received from his parents. He said that when a child is scared, as he was, he can hardly get over it as long as he lives. Probably this was unjust to his parents, for plenty of sermons on hell and purgatory must have contributed to his frightened state of mind. But in any case Martin started out, as a boy, taking the wrath of God very much in earnest and standing in deadly dread of it.

In studying Martin Luther we must never forget that we are talking about a man who lived more than four hundred years ago. All sorts of ideas were believed then that no longer prevail today. For example, the woods and waters—and in Mansfield, especially the mines—were thought to be peopled by fairies, witches and devils. When plagues came, or devastating storms and floods, demons were blamed. To Luther's mother such ideas were the commonplace of her daily life, and when she missed eggs, milk or butter from her larder she thought that devils had stolen them. To his dying day Martin himself held such ideas, as did his whole generation. "Many regions are inhabited by devils," he remarked once. "Prussia is full of them and Lapland of witches." He even described a lake near his native home into which, if a stone were thrown, a storm would rise over the whole countryside, because in that lake captive demons were imprisoned.

We must make up our minds, therefore, that, while we are talking about a man who helped create the modern world, he himself lived in a very ancient world. Martin was a nine-year-old schoolboy when Columbus discovered America. He probably did not hear of that discovery until sometime after it happened, and we have no reason to suppose that it ever made much of an impression on him one way or another. The discovery of even a new hemisphere did not seem *too* important to the citizens of Mansfield, in a world which was soon coming to an end anyway when Christ returned to judge mankind.

As for astronomy, Martin was taught that the earth stood still and that the sun went around it. Everybody then believed that. Young Luther in Mansfield, swallowing everything his teachers said about the stationary earth and the revolving sun, never dreamed that over in the University of Cracow, in Poland, was another studious youth, named Copernicus—ten years older than Luther—who was to change man's whole idea of the universe. For Luther and Copernicus were contemporaries—two brave, pioneering spirits, each one destined in his own realm to upset the established order. When years later, however, Copernicus' book was published, proclaiming that the earth revolves about the sun, Luther, like almost all of his generation including even its greatest thinkers, never believed a word of it. He called Copernicus a "fool, who wishes to revolutionize the whole science of astronomy." He argued that the Bible says that Joshua commanded the sun to stand still, not the earth. He thought *that* proved it was not the earth that moved, but the sun.

So Martin Luther was a child of his own generation, sharing its ancient views, as we doubtless would have shared them had we lived then. But there was something else in Luther the consequences of which no one could have guessed when he was young. Although he was a lusty, vigorous boy, hard-working and with a good mind, jovial and full of fun, he was serious too—sometimes desperately serious about religion. He was destined to change the religious life of the Western world, and how he came to do it makes a fascinating story.

2
Martin
Gets an
Education

AFTER his early school-
ing at Mansfield young Luther was naturally expected
to take up mining, but apparently he tried it, did not
like it, and proved to be a poor hand at it. At any
rate, in later life he confessed that he was not good at
mining. Apparently, too, his parents saw unusual
ability in him which might make possible a more
distinguished career than mining offered. So, when
he was thirteen years old, instead of being kept at
home to help support the family, he was sent away

to school in the town of Magdeburg. A year later he went to a still better school at Eisenach.

His father began to cherish a definite ambition for his promising son. He would become a lawyer. If only he had the stuff in him to make a good lawyer, who could tell how far that might carry him in social status and financial gain? He might even become a legal adviser to the counts of Mansfield, and that was the high point then in Hans Luther's dreams about his son.

It is strange now to think how important a day that was in history when Martin Luther said good-bye to his family, shouldered his pack with all his worldly goods in it, picked up his walking stick and, along with his friend, John Reinicke, started off on his fifty-mile hike to Magdeburg. He took almost nothing with him from home except his family's good will, for in that household money was scarce. Moreover, students away at school in those days were supposed to get their own food in a way that would seem shocking to us. They begged for it. That was the common custom. Groups of schoolboys walked the streets singing, and in return were given hand-outs by the citizens. Martin's singing thus stood him in good stead. He had an unusually strong, delightful voice, and both in Magdeburg and during his early days in Eisenach he largely earned his keep by singing in the streets.

In Eisenach, however, his magnetic personality, along with his captivating voice, brought him an unusual piece of good fortune. Frau Cotta, mother of a well-to-do family, was charmed with this buoyant youngster with the attractive eyes and voice. She heard him sing in the church choir and in the streets, and at last she took him into her own home and became in effect his foster mother. From more than one point of view this was a godsend to Martin. Not only did he have relief from all fear of hunger—for in Magdeburg he had sometimes been hard put to it to get enough to eat—but he found himself in a home where for the first time in his life he lived with refined, cultured gentlefolk.

This point needs emphasis, if one is to understand Luther. He had had a rough upbringing. His home-

Frau Cotta was charmed with Luther's singing

folk were stout characters, but polished manners and
the social graces had not been part of their rugged
heritage. Luther never escaped the consequences of
that fact. There was always a tough side to him; he
could be boisterous, crude, uncouth. His whole gen-

eration was accustomed to using coarse and vulgar language of a kind that would not be permitted in decent circles now, and Luther was no exception. He was going out later on to fight one of the most formidable battles any man ever undertook, and this rough, sturdy quality in him had its valuable uses. Speaking of himself, Luther once said, "God uses coarse wedges for splitting coarse blocks." In Frau Cotta's household, however, he saw another side of life—a cultured, well-bred family with good manners, a delightful social life, parties, dances, plenty of fun and affection along with graciousness and courtesy. Three years of this life in Eisenach was good for Martin. When in later days he had to deal not only with the common people from whom he sprang but with princes and nobles, merchants, educators and distinguished leaders in Church and state, he knew his way around.

Moreover, in Eisenach he found one of the best teachers he ever studied under, John Trebonius. A good schoolteacher, like a good poet, is born, not made, and Trebonius was born for teaching. His attitude toward his students—most unusual in that day of rough methods in the schoolroom—is indicated by the fact that whenever he came into the presence of his pupils, he took off his scholar's cap and bowed, and made all his teachers do the same. Who could tell, he used to say, what distinguished mayors, chancellors, scholars and rulers of the future might be sitting on those benches!

So, Martin flowered out in Eisenach. His school work was excellent, especially in language and literature. His father was delighted. Martin, thought Hans Luther, undoubtedly could become an able lawyer and, since the financial condition of the family was steadily improving, he offered his son, now seventeen, a thrilling opportunity. Martin could go to the University of Erfurt, at that time the greatest university in Germany.

Martin began his collegiate training with a high heart. As his fellow-students at Erfurt saw him, he was a gay, sociable, talkative young fellow. He was naturally witty and companionable. His father sup-

24

plied him with sufficient funds to put him at ease. He dressed in gay clothing, and wore a sword at his side, as was the custom of students at that time. And, like collegians then and now, he bragged about his university. He said once in later years that in comparison with it other universities were no more than primary schools.

Erfurt was a prosperous city and the university was its special pride. For collegiate celebrations the whole town turned out. Young Luther thought he had never seen anything more stirring, especially at commencement, when the successful graduates were escorted through the streets with music and banners and were greeted by shouts from the crowd. Anything with music accompanying it always stirred Luther. Once at Erfurt he had an accident which kept him in his quarters for a while. Finding one of the students' old lutes, he taught himself to play it. That proved to be a source of satisfaction to him as long as he lived. With his lute he entertained his friends and led their singing. In solitude as well—when he was tired or in a discouraged mood—he took up his lute and played a cheerful tune. This love of music lasted all his life. "Music is a delightful and noble gift of God," he used to say. "It has often excited and moved me so that it quickened me to preach."

As for his studies, he worked hard, taking his Bachelor of Arts degree in his nineteenth year and his Master of Arts degree in his twenty-second. On the latter occasion he stood second in a class of seventeen. Then he headed for the law school at Erfurt, and all his father's ambitions for him seemed certain of fulfillment. Hans Luther was overjoyed. He presented Martin with a copy of *Corpus Juris,* the best law book obtainable and very expensive in those days, and had dreams for his son of a high legal position and, as Martin himself said, "a respectable and wealthy marriage."

Something, however, was going on inside young Luther that his father did not know about. He was deeply concerned about religion, and to him that meant anxiety about the wrath of God and the coming judgment, about hell and purgatory, and about how one could save one's soul from the horror of those future torments. His old childhood fears were still profoundly troubling him. He still saw in imagination that stained-glass window in the church at Mansfield, and the altarpiece too, picturing a ship sailing toward heaven with only priests and monks on board, and with common men and women drowning in the sea save for a few rescued by ropes thrown to them by the holy men. Could he be saved if he became a lawyer, married a rich woman, and sought rank and station in the wicked world? That question haunted him. Would he not be tempted and fall, live for money, share in the shyster practices of public life, and end in hell? At this stage of his life Martin was a tormented soul. And the more he thought about it, the more it seemed to him that the only way to solve his problem was to enter a monastery, become a monk, and so escape the evil world and achieve the holy life that would fit him for heaven.

Such was his state of mind when, in the summer of his twenty-second year, after a few weeks as a law student, he made a visit to his Mansfield home and then started to walk back to Erfurt. On the way a tremendous thunderstorm crashed down on him. The lightning was terrific and one flash of it struck near him, causing him to throw himself upon the ground, stunned and frightened. At that moment all his fears of death came to their climax and all his secret broodings about entering a monastery were shocked into decision, and he cried out, "Saint Anne, help me! I will become a monk."

A few days afterward he gave a farewell dinner to his student friends. When he told them his decision they were aghast. They protested against it and pleaded with him, using every argument and appeal they could think of, but in vain. On the morning of the seventeenth of July, 1505, young Luther entered the Augustinian monastery in Erfurt.

So far his father had not heard of what was happening. As Martin wrote him afterward, "I did it without telling you, and against your will." That last phrase puts the matter very mildly. When the staggering news reached Hans Luther that his son had

He cried, "Saint Anne, help me! I will become a monk."

thrown up his promising legal career and entered a monastery, he was broken-hearted. Moreover, he was furious. He would not allow this catastrophe to happen! He came to Erfurt to plead with Martin, but the young man was resolute. In that encounter two strong wills met in head-on collision and Hans could get nowhere with his son. The break between the two was deep and serious. Hans's sorrow was shattering and his anger was hot. It looked at first as though there never could be any reconciliation. Indeed, it took a very sad situation to heal the break at all. The plague—one of those dreadful epidemics of which no one then knew the cause—swept the country, and two of Hans Luther's younger sons died. To make matters worse, the rumor reached Mansfield that Martin had died too. When Hans Luther heard that the rumor was false and that Martin was still alive, his heart softened. He had lost two sons; he would keep his fatherly ties with his eldest boy, even if he was a monk. So Hans relented enough to take up friendly relations again with Martin, but in secret his vexed disapproval never ceased.

Meanwhile young Luther was going through his preparatory year of stern discipline in the monastery and in September, 1506, he became a full-fledged Augustinian monk.

3

Martin
Tries to
Save His Soul

WHEN Martin entered the monastery he was not thinking about reforming the Church or changing the world; he was thinking about himself and about living a holy life that would prepare his soul for heaven. Stepping from the freedom of the university, with its gaiety and jovial fellowship, he entered a strange, new world when he became a monk. But he never did things by halves; he always threw himself headlong into anything he undertook. And now that he was out to save his soul by being a monk, he went to work on it with gusto and determination.

He accepted the rules of monastery life with humble obedience. Prayers in the chapel came seven times a day, one of the services at two o'clock in the morning. Almost everything a monk did was regulated by a schedule that left him little, if any, individual choice—not simply religious duties such as prayers and the reading of sacred books, but also how to stand, walk, dress and eat. Everything was carefully prescribed. Martin was by nature such a vigorous, strenuous, independent person that it is difficult to imagine him fitting cheerfully into this enforced routine, but he did it, at least at first, with zest and relish. Years afterward, however, when he looked back, he was disgusted with it. "The monks," he said, "sought to try one's obedience by requiring that unreasonable, burdensome, childish and foolish things be done with willing and joyful hearts."

One part of his duties must have been especially distasteful—begging for bread. For the Augustinian monks were "mendicants"—that is, they expressed their humility by putting sacks on their backs and begging for food from door to door. Martin had done that as a schoolboy, but for a Master of Arts from the university to walk as a mendicant through the streets of Erfurt, which he so lately had paraded in gay clothing, must have been humiliating. Indeed, one of Luther's early biographers says that the university itself did not like it and persuaded the monastery to let Martin do his begging in neighboring villages. Apparently there was some jealousy of Martin among the monks on this matter of begging. He should not be let off from anything, they thought, just because he was a brilliant student. "My cloister brothers," Luther once said, "were annoyed at me because I was a student. They said, 'As with me, so with thee! Put a sack on his neck!' "

Nevertheless, he was out to save his soul by being a good monk, and he not only did all that was required but made up stiffer requirements of his own. Sometimes he fasted for three successive days, eating not a single thing. He forced himself night after night to go without sleep, and he set periods of prayer for himself far in excess of those called for by the monastery's rules. Once in winter he even refused to use the blankets provided him and nearly froze to death. In all this he was typically Luther: he did nothing moderately, but plunged into everything he undertook with more than wholehearted zeal. Years afterward, when his days as a monk were far behind him, he said, "If ever a monk gained heaven by his monkery, I must have done so. All the brethren who knew me will bear me witness. For I should have martyred myself if I had kept it up longer, with watching, praying, reading and other labors."

Indeed, Luther's extreme self-denials and self-punishments—he even flogged himself—brought him a growing reputation as a very holy man, and the authorities at the monastery decided that he must become a priest. So the day came when he was to say his first Mass. This was a very sacred occasion. According to Roman Catholic doctrine, both then and now, when the priest utters the words of consecration in the Mass, the bread of the Lord's Supper becomes the very body of Christ and the wine becomes the very blood of Christ. Luther stood in awe at the idea that he should be the instrument for working such a miracle, and with mingled fear and expectation he looked forward to the great day when he would officiate at his first Mass.

Above all else he wanted his father there. So Hans Luther, then a well-to-do man, came in style with twenty horsemen accompanying him and, in addition, made a generous contribution of money to the monastery. Hans was doing his best to forget his old resentment about Martin's becoming a monk. After the Mass was over, however, and Martin, who had almost had a panic during the ritual, sat down to dinner with his father, he pressed Hans too far. "Dear father," he said, "why were you so contrary to my becoming a monk? Perhaps you are not quite satisfied even now. The life is so quiet and godly."

This was more than Hans could take. His old rebellion flared up again and he said in a loud enough voice so that the company could hear, "You learned scholar, have you never read in the Bible that you should honor your father and mother? And here you have left me and your dear mother to look after ourselves in our old age."

Poor Martin was badly upset by this and tried to argue that, during the thunder and lightning when he made his decision, it was a voice from heaven that had called him to be a monk. At which Hans grumbled, "God grant it was not an apparition of the devil!"

One wonders how early in his years at the monastery some such doubt as Hans had expressed about his calling began to trouble Martin himself. If doubts did arise, however, he smothered them. And when the head of the monastery ordered him to continue his university studies so that he could serve as a teacher, he threw himself into the task with enthusiasm.

One of the first indications we have that doubts were beginning to disturb Luther's mind appeared on his trip to Rome. A dispute had arisen among the Augustinian monasteries which required settlement by the Pope, and Luther was chosen as one of the two delegates who were to go to the Holy City. They walked all the way, one behind the other, murmuring their prayers as they trudged along, and finding their food and lodging in the monasteries, which were plentiful along the principal roads. They spent five months on the journey, with four weeks of the time in Rome. In later years Luther often spoke of this trip and of the things that most interested him. He loved the hospitality of the southern Germans and the good roads in Switzerland. He found Italian life much more cultured and elegant than the comparatively crude and uncouth life of Saxony. He marveled at the better methods of agriculture in Italy and at the size of the grapes and peaches there, and he enjoyed the flowing smoothness of the Italian language in comparison with his more rough and guttural German. He was full of praise for Italian hospitals and orphanages, which were much better equipped and managed than any he had ever seen. And when at last he came within sight of the sacred city he was thrilled, threw himself on his knees and cried out with all his heart, "Hail, holy Rome!"

Nevertheless, before he was through he was

troubled by many things in Rome that were not holy. To be sure, numberless sacred relics were to be found in the city—a piece of Moses' burning bush, three hundred pieces of the children whom Herod slew in Bethlehem, the chains that bound St. Paul, one of the coins that Judas took for betraying Jesus, a twelve-foot beam on which Judas hanged himself, and countless others. Luther was still a loyal monk; he did not question the stories about these relics, and he venerated them in the belief that such reverence would help to save him from purgatory. Years afterward he exclaimed, "O, dear God, what did I not believe! Everything seemed true, and nothing was so preposterous or false that I did not accept it gladly."

Some things, however, bothered him—especially what seemed to him the frivolity of the priests in Rome. These, he complained afterward, would rattle through six or seven Masses while he was saying one, and, impatient at his serious pace, would say to him, "Get a move on! Get a move on!" Moreover, there was shameful wickedness in Rome, not only among the plain citizens but among the priests and monks too, and Luther heard some bad stories about them. Even Pope Alexander VI had lived a dreadful life, which Roman Catholic historians frankly call an unspeakable disgrace.

Still Luther went on doing all the pious things that a loyal monk was supposed to do in Rome, and one day he climbed a sacred staircase which was said to have come from the palace of Pilate, the Roman governor in Jerusalem who condemned Jesus to be crucified. He climbed the stairs on hands and knees; he said the Lord's Prayer on each step; and then he kissed the step he was kneeling on. That, he was told, would help deliver some soul from purgatory, and he centered his attention on releasing his grandfather, Heine. Then when the stairs were all climbed and the performance was all over, he stood up and said to himself, "Who knows whether it is really so?"

Nevertheless, Luther returned home from Rome still a loyal monk, and there he faced a change that profoundly influenced his whole life—he was transferred from the monastery in Erfurt to the monastery in Wittenberg. Only a small town of some two thousand inhabitants, Wittenberg was the residence of a very important prince, Frederick, Elector of Saxony, and a few years earlier Frederick had founded a new university there, concerning which he had great ambitions. Luther had taught there for one term before he went to Rome, and now he was settled there to stay for the rest of his life. Outwardly he threw himself into his work as a teaching monk with his usual enthusiasm, but inwardly he was still having a dreadful time trying to save his soul. Among the practices supposed to help in achieving that, one of the most important was confessing one's sins to a priest. Then, as now, all faithful Roman Catholics went to the confessional, told the priest in private everything bad they had done which they could remember, and, professing contrition and purpose of amendment, received forgiveness. So Luther ransacked his memory for every wrong thing he could recall that he had done or thought, and then confessed to the priest. Sometimes he did this every day. Once, at least, he spent six hours confessing. He dug up so many trivial deeds to confess that the priest became impatient.

Fortunately for Luther, the priest to whom he confessed at Wittenberg was Johann von Staupitz, Vicar-General of the Augustinian order, who became one of Luther's best friends. Dr. Staupitz was puzzled about Luther. The young man was still terribly afraid of God. When he thought of God, he thought of God's wrath, of his judgments and punishments, and of hell and purgatory. Luther himself said years afterward, "I was myself more than once driven to the very abyss of despair so that I wished I had never been created. Love God? I hated Him."

Dr. Staupitz could not at first make out what was the matter. "Man," he said once, "God is not angry with you. You are angry with God. Don't you know that God commands you to hope?"

Dr. Staupitz was one of the best influences that ever came into Luther's life. Little by little he got Luther to have faith in God's mercy and to trust His goodness instead of being frightened by His wrath. And then Dr. Staupitz did something that started Luther on his great career. He was worried about this promising young man. He saw rich possibilities in him.

He saw that all this morbid fear of Luther's and all these endless, self-punishing endeavors to be an extremely pious monk were getting him nowhere. This young fellow's attention must be turned to something else, he thought. So, one day under a pear tree—Luther never forgot that pear tree—Dr. Staupitz told Luther that he must take his Doctor's degree, and then start in preaching and become Professor of Bible at the university. Luther was stunned. He said afterward that he brought up fifteen arguments to prove that he could not do it. "You are trying to kill me!" he cried. "I would not live three months."

"Quite all right," said Dr. Staupitz. "God has plenty of work for clever men to do in heaven."

So Luther obeyed orders. He took his Doctor's degree, became Professor of Bible at the university, and began to preach. That was the beginning of the great Luther who changed the world. "If it had not been for Dr. Staupitz," said Luther years later, "I should have sunk in hell."

4

The
Big Battle
Begins

L UTHER was not yet thirty years old when he became a full-fledged Doctor of Theology and began his professorship at the univer-sity and his preaching in a local parish church. He never dreamed then what a stormy voyage he was starting on, and had he known what lay ahead, "ten wild horses," as he later said, could not have dragged him into it. At first, however, everything looked promising and hopeful.

Luther turned out to be a great preacher. In the

beginning he was terrified at the thought of speaking in public, but since he had to do it he went at it hammer and tongs, as he always did everything. He paid no attention to the dry-as-dust ways of preaching that were common. He talked to plain people in the plain language they used in everyday life. "I preach as simply as I can," he said, "that common men, children and servants may understand; for the learned already know it all, and I do not preach for them." His sermons were full of pictures drawn from ordinary life; his language was racy, vivid and sometimes violent; he said what he really thought and he said it hard; and his style was conversational as though he were talking to individuals and not to a crowd. The people of Wittenberg had never heard such sermons, and before long he was appointed to preach regularly in the main church of the city.

Meanwhile, Luther was making such an impression that all sorts of responsibilities were laid on him. When he was only thirty-one he was made superintendent of all the monks in his district and had to look after the affairs of eleven monasteries. He was a tremendous worker, and his life now was not at all what it had been in the days when he was trying to save his soul by starving, flogging and freezing himself. He was so busy that he complained once, "Rarely do I have time to observe the hours of prayer, or to say Mass."

Most of all, Luther gave himself to his teaching in the university. He became the most popular professor there, but what he was teaching his students was no more important than what he was teaching himself. For he was lecturing on the Bible and was seeing in it things he had never seen before. We take the Bible for granted; it is our best-selling book, and copies of it are everywhere. We must remember, however, that Gutenberg, who invented printing with movable type, had died only fifteen years before Luther was born. The first book printed on the Gutenberg press had been the Bible, but while it was available for scholars in Luther's time, he himself tells us that he never even saw a complete copy of the Scriptures until he chanced upon one in the library at Erfurt, in his twentieth year. It was not mainly the Bible which was taught even to priests and monks, but rather the writings of the old Church fathers, such as St. Augustine's books. Indeed, when Luther was a monk at Erfurt one of his teachers had said to him, "Brother Martin, let the Bible alone! Read the old teachers; they give you the whole marrow of the Bible; reading the Bible simply breeds unrest."

Now, however, a new day was dawning and Luther's business at Wittenberg was to teach the Bible. So he plunged into it, and learned Hebrew and Greek so that he could read it in its original languages. Especially in St. Paul's Letter to the Romans he found ideas that changed his whole life. Here was a brave and radiant man, St. Paul, who believed in God's mercy, who himself was sure his sins were forgiven, who had found peace and joy because by faith he had accepted Christ as his Saviour. And yet neither in the Letter to the Romans, nor in any letter he wrote was St. Paul concerned about sacred relics, religious pilgrimages, confession to a priest, purgatory and how to get out of it, acts of penance, and all the self-punishments familiar in the monasteries. Luther did not at first dream of denying that these things might have their good uses, but he was certain of one fact: it was not these things that saved the soul. Deep down inside himself a man could find forgiveness and peace simply by accepting God's mercy revealed in Christ. So Luther threw away the old fears which had haunted him from childhood. He was a new man from then on. "Thereupon I felt myself to be reborn," he said, "and to have gone through open doors into paradise."

At first Luther had not the faintest idea where all this was going to lead him, but one can see the effect in some of his sermons. He began preaching simple faith in Christ as the one thing most necessary, and he began attacking practices in the Church that seemed to him to deny that and to be foolish and superstitious—such as going on long pilgrimages to sacred places, for example. Luther exploded against things like that. "Let anyone go on a pilgrimage who feels compelled to," he preached, "but let him learn that God can be served at home a thousand times better by giving the money the journey would cost to the poor, or to wife and children." On some Sundays he let fly his indignation at the foolish and evil ways in which many people prayed to the saints. All good Roman Catholics venerated the saints, and Luther, a loyal Roman Catholic himself, did not mind *that* if it were rightly done. The saints had been unusually good men and women, and if one honored them because of that and tried to become more like them, that was all right with Luther. But in those days one saint was supposed to be especially able to protect people against fire, another against the plague, another against lightning, another against toothache, another against eye trouble, and so on. People prayed to the saints, complained Luther, only when they wanted to get something for themselves by a kind of magic. "We honor the saints," he said in one sermon, "and call upon them only when we have a pain in our legs or our heads, or when our pockets are empty."

Luther had found out that what really matters in religion is what happens deep down inside a man when he has faith in Christ so that his life is changed, and he grew more and more disgusted with many of the Church's practices in which the people put their trust.

Then the day came when Luther stood up in the pulpit and attacked "indulgences." No one can understand Luther's life without knowing what indulgences meant in his generation. The idea began very simply. When a Catholic sinned he confessed to a priest and, if the priest was assured of the penitent's sincere contrition and sincere determination to amend his life, he received forgiveness. Then, however, the priest imposed on the forgiven sinner certain penalties suited to the seriousness of the sins confessed. These "penances," as they were called, took many forms— from prayers and pilgrimages to gifts of money for charity. They were the outward and visible sign of the sinner's sorrow for the wrong done and sometimes, when the sin was serious, they extended over years. What the Church could thus impose as a penalty for sin, however, the Church could also remit, and this freeing of the sinner from his penance was called an indulgence. During the Crusades, for example, the Pope granted indulgence to soldiers who embarked on the holy war, freeing them from all the penalties which they would have undergone had they remained at home and performed the penances which the priest had imposed on them.

In Luther's day, however, indulgences had come to mean something very different from what they had meant at the start. About the beginning of the thirteenth century some churchmen had begun teaching that Christ and the saints had lived such extra good lives that all this extra goodness had accumulated like a growing balance in a bank. There it was—all this extra goodness of Christ and the saints—making an ever larger treasury in the bank. Then these churchmen said that the Pope had the power to use this accumulated wealth of goodness to help poor sinners. If anyone would do what the Pope said, then the Pope could draw on this huge balance of credit to remit penalties and could even use it to save sinners from purgatory. As anyone can see, this put tremendous power into the Pope's hands. If the Pope said that when a man made a pilgrimage to a sacred shrine, or venerated a sacred relic, or said such and such prayers, some of the accumulated wealth of Christ's and the saints' extra goodness would be put to his credit, his penance would be reduced, and he and his family would spend fewer years in purgatory, then the Pope had power to see that this was done. In Luther's day many loyal Roman Catholics were protesting against this idea, and especially against some of its bad abuses, but none the less the Pope was using it. He claimed the power to say, "Do what I tell you and, no matter what your sins are, I will use some of this great store of extra goodness in my control to let you off from punishment."

The real trouble, which stirred Luther up, came when this power of the Pope was used for mercenary purposes. As the *Catholic Encyclopedia* itself says, "Those who granted indulgences might be tempted to make them a means of raising money: and, even when the rulers of the Church were free from blame in this matter, there was room for corruption in their officials and agents, or among the popular preachers of indulgences." Such preachers seemed to make the Pope say, "If you pay me so much money I will grant you an indulgence." That was an easy way to get money. The Pope had only to say, "Pay me so much and you will escape sin's penalties," and the cash poured in. Many people besides Luther were indignant about this way of extracting money from the pockets of the people. Erasmus, a very great scholar and a loyal Roman Catholic to his dying day, lived in Luther's time and he said once, "The Court of Rome clearly has lost all sense of shame; for what could be more shameless than these continued indulgences."

So Luther attacked the practice from his pulpit in Wittenberg, and he stirred up a hornet's nest. For the Elector Frederick, the powerful prince who ruled Wittenberg, had built up one of the greatest collections of sacred relics in all Germany, and he was making a lot of money for himself and for the Pope out of the indulgences promised all those who venerated the relics and paid the price. That was one of the major ways in which Frederick paid the expenses of his court and of the university. Some of the money so obtained doubtless helped to support Luther. Nevertheless, in sermon after sermon, Luther attacked indulgences, although Frederick did not like it one little bit.

Then something happened that carried Luther's attack outside of Wittenberg and heated up all Germany to the boiling point. It was one of the most important events in Luther's life, and this is the story of it. A young prince, named Albert, was so young that according to the rules of the Church he had no right to be a bishop at all, but nevertheless he already held two bishoprics and he wanted another. The Pope would have to appoint him, and Albert knew that he must pay the Pope a big price for it. So Albert and the Pope bargained about it. Leo X was Pope then, and a modern historian says of him that he was "as elegant and as indolent as a Persian cat." One Roman Catholic historian said that having him in the papacy "was one of the most severe trials to which God ever subjected His Church." Leo was then trying to build St. Peter's Cathedral in Rome and he needed money.

So he and Albert cooked up a scheme. He granted to Albert the right to sell indulgences in his territories for eight years, part of the profits to go to Albert to pay for his third bishopric and the rest directly to Leo to help build St. Peter's.

So Albert started a rousing campaign to sell indulgences. A monk named Tetzel was in charge of it and he proved to be a very successful salesman. He put on a grand show, entering every town he visited with a gorgeous procession, and carrying on a gold-embroidered velvet cushion the written promise of the Pope that anyone who paid the price would save souls from the torments of purgatory. Then, when all the townspeople were gathered together, Tetzel preached to them. Here is a quotation which tradition reports from one of his sermons:

"Consider that all who repent and have confessed and have made their contribution of money will receive complete remission of all their sins. Listen to the voices of your dear dead relatives and friends in purgatory, beseeching you and saying, 'Pity us, pity us! We are in dire torment from which you can redeem us with a small gift.' Do

Luther nailed on the church door a call to a public debate

you not wish to? Open your ears! Hear the father saying to his son, the mother to her daughter, 'We bore you, nourished you, brought you up, left you our fortunes, and you are so cruel and hard that now you are not willing for so little to set us free. Will you let us lie here in flames? Will you delay our promised glory?'

"Remember that you are able to release them, for

As soon as the coin in the

coffer rings,

The soul from purgatory

springs."

Multitudes of the people really believed that sort of thing, and so the money poured in for Albert and the Pope.

Tetzel was not allowed to come into Wittenberg with this campaign, but he did come into a neighboring town, so near that many of the people from Wittenberg crossed the border to hear him and to buy the indulgences. This was more than Luther could stand, and one day he walked up to the doors of the church where he preached and nailed onto them a call to a public debate. This in itself was not unusual. Public debates were thus commonly called for on all sorts of questions. What was unusual was the fact that, along with the call for debate, Luther nailed on the church door ninety-five theses—that is, ninety-five statements as to the reasons why Luther thought that Tetzel's sale of indulgences was an outrage.

Even then Luther never guessed what the result of his act would be. Those ninety-five theses turned out to be like a spark that set off a tremendous explosion.

5

Luther Becomes a National Leader

W HEN Luther nailed those ninety-five theses to the church door he had in mind a debate by the leading scholars of the University of Wittenberg about the sale of indulgences. "It was not my plan or my wish to have them get into general circulation," he said later. He therefore wrote the theses in Latin, which was the language of scholars. But to the surprise of Luther, somebody— we do not know who it was—translated those theses into German and had them printed. "In fourteen days," as Luther said, "the theses ran through all Germany."

The result was uproarious. Some people were so angry at Luther that they said he would be burned at the stake within a month. Many of Luther's friends were thoroughly scared, because they too thought that something like that might happen. "You would write against the Pope?" one friend exclaimed. "What do you hope to accomplish by that? They will not permit it." To this Luther answered, "What if they have to permit it?" All over Germany, however, there were many people who were neither angry at Luther nor scared; they were delighted. Here at last, they thought, was somebody who dared stand up and denounce sellers of indulgences, like Tetzel, who were taking huge sums of money from the pockets of the Germans and were carrying German wealth to Rome. One such delighted man, when he read the theses, exclaimed, "Ho, ho! He is come who will do what is needed."

One reason why Luther's theses caused this uproar was not alone what he said but the way he said it.

When he wrote those theses he was angry, and they reflect his anger. As to his claim that all he wanted was a learned debate by scholars about indulgences, that was doubtless his intention, but all the same he was so indignant that he let fly hard-hitting language which stirred everybody up. And when his enemies began angrily to attack his theses, that made him angrier still, and his explanations of what he meant were even more stormy and dangerous than the theses themselves had been. "I claim that the Pope has no jurisdiction over purgatory," he wrote. "If the Pope does have 'power to release anyone from purgatory, why in the name of love does he not put an end to purgatory by letting everyone out? If for the sake of miserable money he can release uncounted souls, why should he not for the sake of most holy love empty the place?" In those days that was dangerous talk. It was an attack not simply on indulgences but on the power of the Pope. When Leo X in Rome first heard of the theses, the report is that he merely shrugged them off, exclaiming, so tradition says, "A drunken German wrote them. When he is sober he will think differently." All over Germany, however, Luther's indignant words were having their effect. The sale of indulgences was falling off and the stream of money to the Pope was drying up, so at last the Pope began to take Luther seriously.

One reason why many Germans welcomed Luther's attack on indulgences sprang not so much from their religion as from their patriotism. During the medieval age Europe had not been organized in strong, unified nations, but had been split up into small principalities under the separate rule of nobles, knights and bishops. In Luther's time, however, this old system—which we now call feudalism—was coming to an end, and unified nations under the rule of kings were being formed. Already England, France and Spain were united countries under powerful monarchs. Germany had not yet made that change; it was still broken up into many separate principalities under local rulers. Nevertheless, across all these boundary lines German patriotism was growing rapidly. Luther shared that patriotism. "I am the prophet of the Germans," he said, and when he talked about "our Germany" everyone could feel his deep emotion.

Increasing numbers of Germans felt like that also; so, while politically Germany was still split up into small sovereignties under an elected emperor, it was becoming more and more united in spirit. And the stronger this patriotism became, the more the German people resented the way in which their money was being channeled off to Italy. While Tetzel, therefore, at first made a financial success in his sale of indulgences, German indignation was growing hotter and hotter under the surface. Then Luther spoke up—a monk, a professor at a great university, a devout Roman Catholic. He said with stout, stinging words what multitudes of Germans had felt but had not dared to say. One can easily imagine why he met with such a hearty response when he said things like this about the Pope's building St. Peter's Cathedral in Rome with German money:

> "The revenues of all Christendom are being sucked into this insatiable cathedral. . . . Before

71

long all the churches, palaces, walls and bridges of Rome will be built out of our money. First of all we should rear living temples in our souls; next, local churches; and only last of all St. Peter's, which is not necessary for us. We Germans cannot attend St. Peter's. . . . Why doesn't the Pope build the cathedral of St. Peter out of his own money? He is richer than Croesus. He would do better to sell St. Peter's and give the money to the poor folk who are being fleeced by the hawkers of indulgences. If the Pope knew what these salesmen are taking from the people, he would rather that St. Peter's should be in ashes than that it should be built out of the blood and hide of his sheep."

That kind of talk struck a responsive chord all over Germany. There were powerful knights and nobles, like Ulrich von Hutten and Franz von Sickingen, who were not interested in Luther for religious reasons. But when he began hammering at the way Rome was siphoning money out of Germany to Italy, they got behind him. They were what we would call "nationalists." They wanted a strong, united Germany, and when they thought of the Pope they thought of him more and more not as the head of the Church but as a foreign sovereign in Rome who was

In Heidelberg Luther was welcomed as a guest of honor

interfering with German affairs. They were getting angrier and angrier about it. At one point they were even ready to go to war.

So, while Luther was in deadly danger of being burned at the stake, increasing numbers of friends began rallying around him, and the story of why he was *not* burned at the stake makes an interesting tale.

For one thing, Luther was an Augustinian monk and Tetzel was a Dominican monk, and the two orders were rivals. It was natural, therefore, for the German Augustinians to stand up for Luther against Tetzel, and that is what happened. When the storm about the ninety-five theses was just beginning, a convention of the Augustinian order was held in Heidelberg, and Luther was a delegate. His friends warned him not to go. He would be assassinated on the road, they said. Nevertheless, he went—disguised, to be sure, so that he would not be recognized, but walking all the way. When he reached Heidelberg, however, he faced a big surprise. He was welcomed as a guest of honor. The ruling count invited him to dinner and personally conducted him on a sightseeing tour of the city. On every side he was treated with respect and admiration, and when the time came to return home his Augustinian brothers would not let him walk. As Luther joyfully remarked, "I went on foot. I came back in a wagon."

Not only did Luther's German brothers in the

Augustinian order thus rally around him, but the students and faculty at the University of Wittenberg did too. He was immensely popular in his home town. When, therefore, a rival university at Frank-fort-on-the-Oder honored Tetzel with a doctorate in theology, and Tetzel used the occasion to make a slashing attack on Luther, all Wittenberg was up in arms. The students begged, borrowed and bought all the copies of Tetzel's defense of indulgences that they could get their hands on—eight hundred in all—and then, inviting the whole town to see the show, they burned them in a big bonfire, which they called "the funeral of Tetzel's theses."

Moreover, Luther found support not only among the German nationalists and the Augustinians, and among his friends at Wittenberg, but among forward-looking scholars all over Europe. Roman Catholics had never been unanimous about the sale of indulgences. There always had been loyal Catholics who condemned the idea. In the century before Luther lived, John Wessel had written an attack on the practice so much like Luther's that Luther—who read

Wessel's work after his own attack—said, "If I had read his books before, my enemies might have thought that I had borrowed everything from Wessel, so great is the agreement between our spirits." In Luther's time, therefore, there were many scholars who really agreed with Luther, although often they did not dare to say so. Some, however, did dare—especially among the younger men. Philipp Melanchthon is typical of this group. He was a learned scholar, a gentle, cultured, lovable man who probably would have lectured quietly at the University of Wittenberg all his life if Luther had not challenged his courage and waked him up. Philipp Melanchthon was utterly different from Luther. As Luther himself put it:

> "I was born to fight with mobs and devils, and so my books are very stormy and warlike. I must remove trees and stumps, cut away thorns and thickets, and fill up swamps. I am the rough woodsman who must blaze the way and clear the path. But Master Philipp comes along gently and quietly; builds and plants, sows and waters, with joy, according to the gifts God has richly bestowed on him."

76

These two men, so completely different in temperament, became devoted friends. There were many others too, especially among the younger scholars, who never would have dared start the fight but who, when Luther had started it, joined in and backed him up.

Nevertheless, while Luther was surprised and encouraged by all these friends who, for one reason or another, rallied around him, he knew that he was in danger of being burned at the stake, and at times he certainly expected it. When Luther was a boy, Savonarola, a monk in the Italian city of Florence, had bravely tried to reform the Church and stop the dreadful abuses under Pope Alexander VI. Savonarola had strong popular support too; at one time he practically controlled the city. Nevertheless the Pope won and Savonarola was put to death by fire when Luther was fifteen years old.

As for the Pope in Luther's day, he did not dream at first that he could not handle the little, obstreperous monk up in Germany. He began by trying to get the

Augustinian order to suppress Luther, but failed. Then the Pope turned to the Dominicans and ordered Sylvester Prierias, Master of the Sacred Palace at Rome, to answer Luther and squelch him. In three days Prierias tossed off an attack on Luther which he felt sure would finish the business. He took his stand on the proposition that the Pope could not possibly make any mistake when he made an *ex cathedra* pronouncement on matters of faith and morals, and he called Luther all sorts of contemptuous names— saying, for example, that he was a leper with a brain of brass and a nose of iron. Luther, however, came back at him, using language equally strong, and refusing to give way an inch. By this time the Pope had made up his mind to settle the matter once for all. He ordered Luther to appear in Rome within sixty days and stand trial for heresy and disobedience.

That put Luther's fate into the hands of Frederick, the Elector of Saxony, who ruled in Wittenberg. It was his business, under the Pope's orders, to seize Luther and send him to Rome. Frederick was a loyal Roman Catholic. He believed in indulgences. He had one of the most valuable collections of sacred relics in Europe and much of his income was derived from them. But he was a German too. Luther had written in his answer to Prierias, "You make the Pope an emperor in power and violence. The Emperor Maximilian and the Germans will not stand for this." Frederick sympathized with Luther that much anyway. Moreover, he was proud of his university and of Luther, its most popular professor, and he saw the learned faculty of the university rallying on Luther's side. What should he do? He was in dreadful confusion and uncertainty, but at last he made up his mind on one matter: Luther would never have a decent chance to defend himself in Rome. Luther, he decided, must not be sent to Rome. Let the case be tried—he could not prevent that—but let it be tried in Germany! On that point he dug in his heels and refused to budge.

Almost certainly it was that decision which saved Luther from being burned at the stake.

6

Luther's
Troubles
Grow Worse

WHAT Frederick wanted most of all was to have the whole disturbing uproar quieted down. If only Luther, on one side, and the Pope, on the other, could come to some agreement and stop the quarrel—*that* was what Frederick most desired. Luther desired that too. He wanted to be loyal to the Pope. He was utterly surprised when the Pope supported Tetzel. "I was sure," Luther wrote, "that he would condemn Tetzel and bless me. But when I expected a benediction from Rome, there came thunder and lightning instead." Luther did not want to disturb the peace of the Church, and if only the Pope had given him half a chance to keep quiet with a good conscience he would have been delighted. Moreover, not only Frederick and Luther, but the Pope also, wanted the uproar to stop. It was not doing him any good. If only he could have found some way of persuading Luther to calm down, make his obedient submission to Rome and keep still, the Pope would have been happy.

So Frederick hopefully arranged that Luther should go to Augsburg and have a private conference with Cardinal Cajetan. Cajetan was coming to Augsburg anyway for an important "diet"—that is, a convention of the German rulers—and he agreed to see Luther afterward. Luther didn't want to go. His friends told him that the whole arrangement was a scheme to seize him and carry him off to Rome. Luther wrote later that when he started out he saw only death at the stake in store for him, and that he was distressed to think of the disgrace he would bring on his father and mother. Nevertheless, he went, and walked all the way to Augsburg.

The conference with Cajetan did no good at all. The Cardinal was under orders either to make Luther say that he was wrong and that the Pope was altogether right, or else to arrest Luther and bring him to Italy for trial. That threatening method was, of course, exactly the wrong way to approach Luther. It only stirred up his indignation and made him more determined. Either Cajetan himself or one of his retinue—reports differ—stormed at Luther, saying, "Do you think that the Pope cares for the opinions of Germany? Do you think that the princes will take up arms for you? No, indeed! And where will you be then?" To this Luther answered, "In the hands of God." Luther said afterward that Cajetan was no more fitted to manage the affair than an ass is to play a harp. As soon as the interview was over, Luther's friends, fearing for his safety, hurriedly smuggled him out of the city—as Luther wrote, "without trousers, boots, spurs or sword"—and that first day

Luther rode forty miles on horseback to get as far away from Augsburg as possible. So he returned safely to Wittenberg.

Of course, the disappointment about Luther's interview with Cajetan upset Frederick dreadfully. What was he to do now with this troublesome monk? Luther sympathized so much with Frederick's difficulty that he offered to leave Saxony and go somewhere into exile if that would help matters. While, however, as Luther wrote later, "At first the prince would have been willing not to have me here," Frederick now stood his ground and would not let Luther go.

Frederick was one of the most powerful princes in Germany, and for many reasons the Pope did not wish to offend him. So the Pope decided to try to soften his attitude. He sent to Wittenberg a papal chamberlain named Carl von Miltitz. Cajetan had vainly used vinegar on Luther; von Miltitz decided to use molasses. He brought for Frederick the most honorable decoration the Pope could give, the "golden rose," and when he came to Wittenberg he quietly spread the rumor that if Luther would only give in and submit to the Pope, the Pope might make him a bishop. In one of his first interviews with Luther, von Miltitz said to him genially, "We'll have this all fixed up in no time." Indeed, Luther received one letter from one of von Miltitz' companions, saying that he might have almost any honor he desired if he would only surrender to the Pope. And Frederick later said that Luther might even have been made a cardinal if he had been willing to submit.

Moreover, von Miltitz succeeded in touching Luther on a very sensitive spot. He argued that the uproar which Luther had started was hurting the Church. He pled with Luther, for the sake of the Church's peace, to calm down, keep quiet and let the controversy die. Von Miltitz saw that the idea of arresting Luther and taking him to Rome was nonsense. As he reported afterward, out of every four Germans three were on Luther's side and an army of twenty-five thousand men would not be large enough to carry Luther to Italy. He saw, too, that Luther would not recant and confess that he was wrong. So the next best thing was to persuade Luther simply to keep still. For the sake of the peace of the Church, would not Luther keep quiet about indulgences, if his enemies would keep quiet too? Luther agreed to that. He was a hard man to drive but he was an easy man to lead. He agreed to stop shouting if the others would stop shouting too.

For a while it looked as if von Miltitz, who apparently had by-passed Cajetan and exceeded his authority from the Pope, had solved the problem and stilled the storm. This seemed the more possible because the Pope issued a statement condemning some of the worst ideas about indulgences. The statement did not by any means go far enough to suit Luther, but it did seem hopeful. To be sure, in his letters to von Miltitz the Pope called Luther "that child of Satan, son of perdition, scrofulous sheep and harmful weed in the vineyard," but nevertheless the Pope was seriously worried now about the way things were going in Germany, and von Miltitz himself said that Rome would gladly pay ten thousand ducats to end the trouble. In the hope of ending it, Rome even turned against Tetzel. The popular hatred of Tetzel in Germany had become so hot that he had hidden himself away in a monastery in Leipsig. There von Miltitz sought him out, blamed him for the trouble and passed condemnation on him. Tetzel was crushed by this turn of events and he died soon afterward.

For a while all this did soften Luther and make him feel mellow and hopeful. Just as much as von Miltitz, he too wanted peace and quiet. Luther was such a rough, rugged fighter that we naturally emphasize his stormy qualities, but underneath he was a most sociable, good-natured man, full of fun, kindhearted, able to tell endless humorous stories and enjoy uproarious laughter with his friends. He was not just a fighter, for he said once, "My soul is too glad and too great to be at heart the enemy of any man." He even felt sorry for Tetzel and, before the poor fellow died, wrote him a letter in which he said, "Don't take it too hard! You didn't start this racket [of indulgences]. That child had another father."

Above all Luther cared for the Church. He had been brought up as a devout Roman Catholic and he wanted to stay that way. He had seen the best in Roman Catholicism and he loved it. He knew the good lives of the Church's loyal people and the faithful service rendered by conscientious priests and monks. The idea of causing trouble in the Church and especially of differing with the Pope at first horrified him. He did not want to hurt the Church, certainly not to divide it and spoil its unity. He believed in the Pope as the head of the one Church of Christ. All he wanted to do was to rid it of some very wrong things that were being done and that, at first, he was sure the Pope would stop when he knew about them. So Luther, hoping that all would come out well, agreed to keep still.

This lull in the storm, however, did not last long. Luther had promised to keep still if his enemies did—but they didn't. Then Luther blamed himself for having been too soft, and regretted having been deceived by what he called the "Judas kiss and crocodile tears" of von Miltitz. When his enemies started hammering him again, Luther began hammering back, and once more the fight was on.

This renewed battle really started with a debate carried on by printed pamphlets between John Eck, one of the most learned scholars in Germany, and Andreas Carlstadt, a fellow-professor and a friend of Luther's at Wittenberg. Eck had been against Luther from the beginning. He had made a fierce attack on the ninety-five theses, which Luther had answered. It was Carlstadt, however, who took up the cudgels now and went after Eck, and then Eck went after Carlstadt, and the printed discussion continued for months, until at last both sides agreed to have a public, face-to-face debate in Leipsig. Luther was keeping still, as he had promised von Miltitz he would do, but then Eck published a statement of the positions he was going to defend and the positions he was going to attack at Leipsig. That statement made it perfectly clear that the man Eck was really attacking was not Carlstadt but Luther. So, since his enemies did not propose to keep still, Luther did not intend to keep still either. An arrangement, therefore, was made that when Carlstadt went to Leipsig he could take along with him such friends as he chose, and of course he chose Luther. When Tetzel, a disgraced and dying man, heard that Luther had been promised safe conduct to go to Leipsig for the debate, he exclaimed, "If that isn't the very devil!"

That debate at Leipsig was one of the most important events in Luther's life. It was an occasion fraught with danger as well. A group of professors and two hundred students, carrying battle-axes, went from Wittenberg, and an armed bodyguard of seventy-six men was appointed to protect Eck. Obviously nobody trusted anybody and, while there was no real violence attempted, the whole city was tense and the task of keeping order was difficult.

The debate before a large audience went on for eighteen days, and when it was all over Luther was a deeply disturbed man. For Eck was an able scholar and a skillful debater; he knew exactly how to get Luther into trouble, and he succeeded in doing it.

To understand this we must see what had been going on inside Luther's mind. At the beginning, when Luther first attacked indulgences, he had appealed from Tetzel to the Pope, feeling sure that he,

The debate at Leipsig went on for eighteen days

Luther, was right and that the Pope would support him. When the Pope instead condemned him, Luther had to change his position; he appealed, as he said, from the Pope-poorly-informed to the Pope-to-be-better-informed. This was dangerous for it implied that the Pope was mistaken and needed to be taught better. Then, when Luther had presented to the Pope statements based on the Bible which he hoped would cause the Pope to correct himself, and the Pope did not correct himself at all, Luther had to change his position again. This time he appealed from the Pope to a general council of the Church, a great assembly of the Church's scholars and leaders. That was a popular idea in Luther's day. Many loyal Roman Catholics felt that not the Pope alone but the voice of the whole Church, speaking through a council, should decide disputed matters. When, however, Luther was faced with the fact that there had been church councils which had condemned some ideas that Luther had been fighting for, Luther had to change his position again. He had to acknowledge that even a church council could be wrong. "I shall not be moved," he

said to Eck, "until the most excellent doctor proves
that a council cannot make mistakes, has not made
mistakes, and does not make mistakes."

So Luther was in a tight place. He still deeply desired to remain a loyal Roman Catholic, but here he
found himself forced to say that both the Pope and a
church council could be mistaken, and that he had
the right to differ from them. So he had to change his
position again, and this time he appealed from the
Pope and the church councils to the Bible itself. That
was the real authority, he said; every idea is to be
judged right or wrong according to what the Bible
says. But his enemies pounced on that statement, too.
The Catholic Church, they said, also believes the
Bible; it believes the Bible as the Pope understands
and interprets it. What you are doing, they said to
Luther, is claiming that your interpretation of the
Bible is right and that the Pope's interpretation is
wrong. You are really trusting your own reason and
conscience in understanding the Bible, they said, as
against what the Pope says it means.

That was exactly what Luther was doing. And at that point his enemies had him in a trap.

Long before the debate at Leipsig Luther had been wrestling with these dangerous doubts. Deep inside himself he had made up his mind that he did not believe anything just because the Pope or a church council said it was so. What he believed was the truth in the Bible, and he had to believe what he himself honestly thought the Bible said was the truth, even if popes and councils said that the Bible meant something else.

From many things which Luther had previously written Eck could see that this was Luther's real position, and at Leipsig Eck forced Luther to bring it all out into the open. Eck saw that the real issue was not simply whether Luther thought this or that about indulgences; the real issue was whether or not Luther would agree that the Pope and church councils could make no mistakes about matters of faith and morals. So Eck skillfully handled the debate to make Luther come out frankly on that real issue, and Luther did so. "I assert," he said, "that a council has sometimes made mistakes and may sometimes make mistakes. . . ." "A simple layman," he cried, "armed with Scripture, is to be believed above a Pope or a council. . . . For the sake of Scripture we should reject Pope and councils." This, as everyone knows, denies the basic teaching of the Roman Catholic Church, so when the debate at Leipsig was over, Luther had no doubt that he was going to have to face the serious consequences.

These were not long in forthcoming. Eck went to Rome and told the Pope just what had happened and what Luther's position really was, and the Pope did the only thing he could logically do under the circumstances: he issued an official statement—the technical name for it is a "bull"—denouncing Luther as a heretic and an enemy of the Church. In this bull the Pope forbade the reading of Luther's books, called upon Christians everywhere to burn them, and threatened with condemnation anyone who defended Luther or protected him. Further, he announced that if within sixty days after the bull reached Germany

Luther did not repent and confess that he was wrong, he would be excommunicated and driven out of the Roman Catholic Church.

No wonder that Luther came back to Wittenberg a very disturbed man!

7

The
Great Days
at Worms

WHILE Luther was disturbed, however, his fighting spirit was aroused. Whole wagonloads of Luther's books were burned in some of the cities of Germany, but that only made him more determined. When at last the Pope's bull reached Wittenberg, Luther's friends gathered a great crowd of his fellow-professors and students, and Luther publicly burned the bull. That meant his definite break with the Roman Church. Luther said afterward that he did the deed with trembling, but that after it was done he was more satisfied with it than with any other act of his life.

Nobody then could guess how the whole matter was coming out. Certainly Luther's chances looked slim. Not only was the Pope against him, but the Emperor was too. Early in the year when the Leipsig debate was held, the old Emperor Maximilian died. A new one, Charles V, was elected in his place. Charles V had some German blood in his veins and the Germans at first were glad of his election. Charles, however, was at heart a Spaniard and he not only disappointed the Germans on political questions but on religious matters as well. A faithful Roman Catholic, he did not intend to let a poor German monk like Luther get him into trouble with the Pope. So how could Luther, in spite of his many friends, expect to escape, with the Pope and the Emperor both against him?

Moreover, Luther had lost some of his friends by one thing which he had said in the debate with Eck at Leipsig. This had to do with the teachings of a man named Jan Hus, who had been born more than a century before Luther was born. When Hus grew up in the country of Bohemia, just east of Germany, he had attacked what seemed to him the evils in the Roman Church and had said many things exactly like those which Luther was saying. A church council at the city of Constance in Switzerland had summoned Hus to appear before it and had condemned him as a heretic, in consequence of which he was burned at the stake. The Bohemian people, who strongly agreed with Hus, were so angry at his martyrdom that a civil war followed, in which German blood was spilled. Therefore, many Germans feared the very name of Hus and thought of him as one who had caused riot and violence. Eck cleverly made use of this in the debate at Leipsig. He quoted some of the things Hus had said and then exploded at Luther, crying, "You are supporting the pestilent errors of Jan Hus." Luther tried to get out of that trap, but he couldn't, and at last he answered stoutly, "It is certain that among the statements of Jan Hus and the Bohemians are many most Christian and evangelical truths, and these the universal Church cannot condemn." That horrified Luther's enemies and frightened his friends. When he said *that,* Duke George, who was presiding at the debate, swore loudly, and all over Germany Luther's foes began calling him "the Saxon Hus."

So Luther was in a tight place. But throughout his life it was true of him that the tougher the situation he faced, the tougher he became. It was so now. "For me the die is cast," he cried. "I despise alike Roman fury and Roman favor. I will not be reconciled or communicate with them. Let them damn and burn my books!" And, instead of giving in to discouragement and fear when he returned from Leipsig, he had gone to work and had written the three greatest books that ever came from his pen. The first, called *An Address to the German Nobility,* was a rousing call to German rulers to come out on the side of a reformation that would transform their country. The second, called *The Babylonian Captivity of the Church,* was a fearless attack on what seemed to Luther the basic evils in the Roman Church, and especially its ideas of the sacraments. The third, called

The Freedom of the Christian Man, was a stirring plea for liberty and the right use of it. Luther's enemies could not burn these books fast enough to keep them from spreading all over Germany, and by them he made more friends than he had lost.

Meanwhile the sixty days during which the Pope had given Luther time to repent and recant had gone by, and so the Pope excommunicated him, condemning him as a wicked heretic and an enemy of the Church. That, however, did not by itself put an end to Luther, for the Pope could not actually get at him unless the civil government in Germany consented. Everything, therefore, depended on how the Emperor and the political rulers of Germany would act. Now Emperor Charles V, while proposing to be a loyal Roman Catholic, had plenty of differences with the Pope; and with Germany so strongly on the side of Luther and the Pope so strongly against him, Charles did not know what to do. First Frederick, Elector of Saxony, and many other friends of Luther, put heavy pressure on him to give Luther a fair hearing before a German diet. Then Cardinal Aleander, whom the Pope had sent to handle the case, put pressure on him to send Luther to Rome for trial and execution. What to do? First the Emperor gave in to Frederick and very politely invited Luther to appear before him and the German princes at Worms. Then the Emperor gave in to Aleander and canceled the invitation. Then he reversed himself again and renewed the invitation. Would Luther go? Indeed he would! "If I am summoned," he wrote to his friend Spalatin, "I will do what in me lies, to be carried there sick, if I cannot go well. . . . Expect anything of me except flight or recantation. I will not flee, much less recant. So may the Lord Jesus strengthen me!"

Of course the Emperor would have been happy if he could have shipped Luther off to Rome and been done with him, but the situation in Germany made that impossible. Cardinal Aleander, in his reports to the Pope—they are still in existence—made clear what that situation was. Out of every ten Germans, he reported, nine cried "Luther!" and the tenth cried "Death to the Pope!" Legions of noblemen, he said, were enlisted under the leadership of that fiery knight, Ulrich von Hutten, ready to fight the Pope. Many Germans, he wrote, who did not understand what Luther was really driving at, nevertheless supported him because they hated the Pope. Multitudes of the common people, he said, were sure that they could be good Christians and good Catholics too, even if they renounced the Pope and refused longer to be subject to him. As for the princes, like Frederick, they were more and more certain that Luther was right, and Aleander reported Frederick as saying, "Our faith has long lacked this light which Martin has brought to it."

Under these circumstances Luther started for the city of Worms on April 2, 1521, with a promise from the Emperor of safe conduct, coming and going. He traveled in state in a covered wagon. The towns he passed through gave him a rousing welcome, so that Aleander angrily reported that his journey was a triumphal procession. Luther was in a high mood. "The devil saw clearly the mood I was in when I went to Worms," he later wrote to Frederick. "Had

I known that as many devils would set upon me as there were tiles on the roofs, I should have sprung into the midst of them with joy."

About ten o'clock in the morning on April 16th a trumpeter in Worms announced that Luther was arriving, and the whole town turned out to greet him. At four o'clock that afternoon he walked into the great hall of the bishop's palace and faced the Emperor, who was surrounded by a splendid company of noblemen and princes, bishops and archbishops, representatives of the various German states, and even ambassadors from abroad including two from England. Luther entered the hall confident and smiling, which made Aleander furious; and the Emperor, catching his first glimpse of this plain, homely monk, exclaimed, "That fellow will never make a heretic of me."

In the presence of that distinguished assembly, which had the power to condemn him to death, Luther was confronted by a pile of his books, and an archbishop asked him whether he had written them.

He walked into the great hall of the bishop's palace

"The books are all mine," he answered, "and I have written more."

Then the archbishop asked him, "Do you defend them all or do you wish to reject some of them?"

Luther replied, in effect, that this was a serious question, about which to say too little or too much would be dangerous. "I beg you," he said, "give me time to think it over." That answer surprised and irritated the examiners, but the Emperor granted

Luther's request and gave him until the next afternoon to prepare his reply.

On Wednesday, therefore, Luther faced the Emperor again. "You asked me yesterday," he said to the examiner, "whether the books were mine and whether I would repudiate them. They are all mine but, as for the second question, they are not all of one sort." Then Luther divided his writings into three classes. The first, he said, were books about Christian faith and life that even his enemies could find no fault with. Of course he would not repudiate those. The second, he said, were attacks on the evil lives and false teachings of the popes and their supporters, and if he repudiated them the "incredible tyranny" with which the Roman Church was devouring Germany would only be increased and strengthened. He certainly would not repudiate those books. The third, he said, were attacks on individuals with whom he disagreed. He confessed that sometimes, in the heat of his argument, he had used more violent language than was gracious and seemly, but as for repudiating even those books as a whole he would not do it.

Then he made a ringing appeal to the Emperor, warning him not to resist God's will as many an ancient king like Pharaoh had done, and ending with the words, "I cannot escape my duty to my Germans. I commend myself to Your Majesty. May you not suffer my adversaries to make you ill-disposed to me without cause. I have spoken."

This reply, of course, enraged the Pope's party in the assembly, and the archbishop lashed out at Luther with a fierce attack, demanding of him a straight answer to the question: Did he or did he not repudiate his books and the errors they contained? Luther must have known that this was coming, and he was ready with his famous answer. According to the earliest printed report, this is the way the answer ran:

"Since, then, Your Majesty and Lordships demand a simple response, I will give one with neither horns or teeth to this effect. Unless I am convinced by the testimony of Scripture or by clear reason—for I believe neither Pope nor councils alone, since it is certain they have often made mistakes and contradicted each other—my conscience is obedient to the Word of God. I cannot and will not retract anything, for it is neither safe nor right to act against one's conscience. Here I stand, I cannot do otherwise. God help me! Amen."

After that it seemed certain that the assembly would have to condemn Luther. The Emperor was determined to condemn him, and he read a statement to the assembly saying that on that decision "I am resolved to stake my lands, my friends, my body, my blood, my life and my soul." That night, however, a placard was nailed on the door of the town hall and on other doors in Worms. All the placard had on it was a picture of a peasant's shoe. That would have meant nothing to us, but it meant a lot in Germany then. All over Germany and in other countries too the peasants were seething with rebellion, and the peasant's shoe had become their symbol. What the placard nailed on the town hall's door in Worms meant was that if Luther was condemned the peasants would probably revolt. That meant war and bloodshed, assassination and ruined estates. The German princes were frightened. Everything possible, they said, must be done to prevent that catastrophe.

Moreover, Luther had said, as he always said, that if he could be persuaded he was wrong he would be the first to throw his books into the fire. So a committee was appointed to talk with Luther privately, and for a week its members labored with him. They appealed to his patriotism, to his duty to the Emperor, to his care about the peace of the Church. But Luther was adamant. The committee got nowhere with him. He could not be persuaded and he would not say he was wrong.

So at last he was condemned in an edict which made him an outlaw for the rest of his life. To be sure, in the meantime some of the leading princes and noblemen had left Worms, so the edict was signed only by Luther's enemies who had stayed in town. Nevertheless, he stood condemned by the Emperor as well as by the Pope, and he was an outlaw. He was to be arrested wherever found and sent to the Emperor, and it was a crime to read his books or to support and befriend him in any way.

Then Luther disappeared. He simply vanished. Where he was nobody knew. The rumor ran through

Germany that he had been murdered. Up in the Netherlands Albrecht Dürer, the famous artist, who was on a journey there, heard the rumor and exclaimed, "O God, if Luther is dead, who will henceforth explain to us the gospel? What might he not have written for us in the next ten or twenty years!"

Luther, however, was not dead. What had happened was this: Luther had slipped out of Worms and had started back toward Wittenberg in his covered wagon. Then one evening, as he and two companions were driving into the woods near Eisenach, where he had gone to school as a boy, a party of armed horsemen fell upon them and, cursing roughly and acting violently, dragged Luther out and carried him off. Putting him on horseback, they led him around and around through the woods until, late at night, they brought him secretly to Wartburg Castle. There the great doors closed behind him and shut him in.

All over Europe the story went and, of course, almost everyone supposed that Luther's enemies had kidnaped him and perhaps murdered him. On the

The armed horsemen dragged Luther out and carried him off

contrary, the whole scheme had been arranged by Frederick. He was determined to save Luther's life. Against the protests of Luther, who did not like the scheme at all, Frederick had ordered some of his own horsemen to capture Luther and carry him to Wartburg.

So there he was, excommunicated by the Pope and outlawed by the Emperor, and now hidden by his friends in Wartburg Castle with no one for company except the warden and two serving boys.

8

Luther
in
Exile

For nearly a year Luther was kept hidden in Wartburg Castle and its immediate neighborhood. He disguised himself so that no one would recognize him. All monks had shaven heads, but he let his hair grow long and, as well, grew a mustache and a bushy beard, until it was said that his own mother would not know him. He took off his monk's costume and put on the clothes of a knight, wearing a gold chain and carrying a sword. He changed his name to Junker George. He tried to act like a young nobleman and once he went on a two days' hunting expedition with the warden. He did not enjoy it, however. They got only two rabbits and three partridges. It might be all right, he thought, to kill bears, wolves and wild boars, but why kill defenseless rabbits? Indeed, he tried to save one rabbit by hiding it in his sleeve but, as he wrote, "The dogs found the poor beast and bit it through my coat, breaking its leg and strangling it." That was too much for Luther.

Altogether he had a miserable year. "I did not want to come here," he wrote, "I wanted to be in the fight." And once he even said, "I would rather burn on live coals than rot here." Luther never liked to be alone. He always needed companions to keep up his spirits. Especially during that year, of all years, when the struggle which he had started was raging all over Germany and his friends and backers were carrying the burden of it, it was maddening to be holed up in lonely seclusion in Wartburg. He had dreadful times of depression. He wanted to die and have it over with. When news reached him of a friend's death, he wrote, "Would that we too might live no longer!" Doubts and fears troubled him. Had he been right? He thought of all the confusion and turmoil he had caused. Was it worth while? Would any good come out of it? He wrote to one friend, "You can believe that I am exposed to a thousand devils in this lazy solitude." In Wartburg Castle tourists are still shown the room where, so the story runs, Luther actually saw the devil and threw an ink pot at him.

To be sure, at times he found some peace of mind. He would say to himself that he was not there by his own choice, that he was ordered to stay hidden there, that it was God's will and that he could not help it. He would persuade himself that, since he could not be out in the thick of the struggle, the best thing was to forget it. Once he even wrote to his friend Spalatin, "What is going on in the world I care nothing for. Here I sit in quiet." Anyone who understands Luther, however, will realize that he could not long keep up that kind of bluff. He cared more about what was going on in Germany than he cared about his own life.

So, despite the fact that he was holed up in Wartburg Castle, he began getting into the struggle by letter. He wrote continually to his friends in Wittenberg, giving advice and begging for all the news. At first he was delighted by what he heard. Things were going very well. His friends missed him but they were forging ahead, and the reformation of the Church was going strongly forward under the leadership of men like Philipp Melanchthon. Far from making Luther jealous, this pleased him so much that he wrote joyfully to Melanchthon, "Your affairs go better in my absence than when I am present."

Luther's happiness, however, did not last long. The news from Wittenberg began to be troublesome. When Luther had left for Worms, very little had been changed in the day-by-day religious life of the people and in the way the Church's services were run. Even the sale of indulgences had not been altogether stopped. Now, however, changes were taking place thick and fast. Priests who, according to Roman Catholic law, could never marry, were getting mar-

ried; even monks and nuns were leaving their cloisters and marrying; meat was eaten on fast days; the
Mass, which later Protestants were going to call the
Lord's Supper, was being celebrated partly in German instead of all in Latin; not only the bread of the
Mass but the wine also was given to the common
people, which was contrary to Roman Catholic practice; prayers to the Virgin Mary and to the saints
were being discouraged; the sacred statues and
images in the churches were being smashed; and in
one detail after another the familiar forms of worship
were being altered. All this caused an uproar. Some
wanted the changes to be made even more rapidly;
others were angry and upset because the changes
were coming so fast. As Spalatin said, "What a mess
we are in!"

Luther was so disturbed that he slipped away from
Wartburg and made a secret trip to Wittenberg. It
was a brief trip, and he returned feeling a little more
comfortable about the situation. But he was troubled,
and well he might have been, for as the weeks went

by things got worse instead of better, and Frederick and all his leading citizens were becoming desperately anxious.

In the meantime, while all this was going on, Luther was at work in Wartburg Castle on one of the most important tasks he ever undertook. He translated the whole New Testament into German. To be sure, eighteen translations of the Bible into German had been made before that, but they had all been translations from the Latin Bible which the Roman Catholic Church officially used and, consequently, the German rendering was stiff and formal —not at all the kind of German that the common people used in daily speech. Luther translated the New Testament directly from the original Greek, and he set himself to put it into the kind of language that plain people understood and used. "You must not get your German from the Latin, as these asses do," he said, "but you must get it from the mother in the home, the child in the street, the common man in the market place." Later Luther translated the Old Testament from the Hebrew language in the same

Luther translated the New Testament into German

way. He did it so well that even now, more than four hundred years afterward, Luther's German translation of the Bible has never been equaled.

So the months went by, with the news from Wittenberg growing ever more disturbing. The Elector Frederick, along with wise leaders in the Church like Melanchthon, tried to keep the situation steady, but, as Melanchthon put it, "The dam has broken, and I cannot stem the waters." Violence broke out. The statuary in the churches was destroyed by mobs who denounced the images as idols before which the people prayed. Stones were thrown at those who said their prayers at the shrines of the Virgin Mary. Rioting students broke up church services where they thought changes to the new order of things were not being made fast enough, and once at least they even dragged the priest from the altar. And then some very revolutionary radicals from the town of Zwickau invaded Wittenberg, claiming that they were prophets and had direct orders from God as to what should be done. They brushed aside the Bible as unimportant and relied only on what they claimed God privately told them. They denounced education, claiming that God spoke mostly to those who had not been spoiled by going to school. They announced that soon all the ungodly folk were going to be slain either by the Turks or by the godly people themselves. These wild fanatics were so sure of themselves that they made a strong impression in Wittenberg, and the confusion grew worse and worse.

Luther could not stand it any longer. Frederick told him he must not come back, but he had to come back. At last the town council in Wittenberg, despite Frederick, invited him back, and back he came. That was one of the bravest things he ever did. He had been excommunicated by the Pope and outlawed by the Emperor, and even Frederick did not see how he could save Luther if he returned. Nevertheless, while he stood in the deadliest danger he ever was in, it was a glad day in Luther's life when he turned his back on Wartburg Castle and headed for home.

On the way he stopped at the Black Bear Inn at Jena and there ran into two Swiss students who were going to the University of Wittenberg. One of them,

John Kessler, afterward wrote the story of what happened. Luther was still disguised as Junker George. When the two students came into the inn, he was sitting alone at a table reading a book, and he cordially invited them to join him and have a drink. He was so friendly, wrote Kessler, that they accepted his invitation, and told him who they were and where they were going. Then they said to him, "Do you know, sir, whether Martin Luther is now at Wittenberg, or where he is?"

"I have trustworthy information," Luther replied, "that he is not there at present, but will be soon."

At that news the boys exclaimed, "Thank God! We are determined, if our lives are spared, to see and hear Luther. For we undertook this journey on his account."

Then Martin, who was evidently enjoying the conversation, asked the boys, "What do they think of Luther in Switzerland?"

"There are many opinions, sir, as everywhere else," one of the boys answered. "Some cannot praise him enough, and they thank God that truth has been revealed and error exposed through him. But some damn him as an intolerable heretic, particularly the clergy."

At this Luther remarked, "I can well imagine that it is the clergy."

For some reason the landlord of the inn had guessed that Junker George was really Martin Luther, and he called one of the boys aside and told him so. But the boy thought he was joking and exclaimed, "Oh, come, Mr. Landlord, you wish to play the fool with me!" So, after a pleasant evening the party at the inn broke up. Imagine, then, the surprise of those boys when the next Saturday they called on the proper official at the University of Wittenberg to present their letters of introduction, and there before their astonished eyes was Martin Luther, looking just as he had at Jena. "He greeted us with a laugh," wrote John Kessler, and he then introduced them to Philipp Melanchthon and other professors who were there.

Luther's return to Wittenberg, however, was no laughing matter. It is sometimes a good deal easier to start a fire than it is to control it after it once gets started. That was Luther's problem now. He had started a reformation of the Church that was spreading widely over Germany, but it was getting badly out of hand. Hitherto he had had enemies to fear—and there were plenty of them left—but now he faced cranks and hotheads who called themselves his friends but who were giving his movement a bad name. He even said that these hotheads were doing his cause more harm than the Pope and all the Pope's supporters could do.

So he was determined to clean up the situation in Wittenberg and bring order out of chaos, and he never showed his character and ability to better advantage. By the sheer force of his personality he took control of the town. Beginning on the Sunday after his return he preached to great crowds in the city church for eight successive days. He talked common sense to them. He said that what mattered in Christianity was what happened deep inside people when by faith in Christ and humble obedience to Him their characters and lives were changed. He said that outside matters like sacred statues, the use of German or Latin in the Mass, the way church services were conducted, and all such externals, were not of first importance. He said that both the people who were upsetting everything by sudden changes and the people who were frightened by the changes were wrong. Exercise moderation, he said. To use violence in reforming religion was wicked nonsense. Only patience and good will would ever accomplish anything. "Give men time," he said in one sermon. "It took me three years of constant study, reflection and discussion to arrive where I now am. Can the common man, uninstructed in such matters, be expected to move the same distance in three months?"

So Luther calmed the storm in Wittenberg.

The effect of this was felt all over Germany. Multitudes of the Germans—especially the poor people, the oppressed underdogs—were seething with rebellion, not only against the old Church but against all sorts of tyranny and injustice. Violent revolt and even civil war were threatening. And here was Luther, standing out against violence, pleading for good order against anarchy, and proving himself able to control the dangerous situation as no one else could. So Luther became the one most necessary man in Germany. Even those who did not like him began to depend on him. When, therefore, another assembly of the German rulers was held at Nürnberg, and the Pope urged the rulers to enforce the edict against Luther which they had agreed to at Worms, they refused. They said that each prince could do as he

He was driven from one town "with stones and mud"

pleased about it. So Luther was safe in Saxony and the door was opened for his reformation of the Church to go forward in any part of Germany where the local ruler was favorable to it.

After that, in one town after another, Luther's ideas were accepted, and reforms were made in the practice of the churches that changed them from being Roman Catholic toward being what we now call Protestant. Moreover, the leaders in all such towns naturally turned to Luther for advice. He found himself, without intending it, becoming the chief counselor and overseer of the churches all over Germany which favored his reforms. To be sure, he faced plenty of opposition. His old friend Carlstadt, who wanted the changes made more rapidly, turned against him in disgust; and from at least one town, Orlamünde, where the violent hotheads were in control, he was driven, so he wrote, "with stones and mud," and with people yelling at him, "Get out, in the name of a thousand devils, and break your neck before you leave!"

Nevertheless, it was clear that on the whole Luther was winning, and that what we now call the Protestant Reformation was going forward at a pace which neither Pope nor Emperor could stop.

9

The
Protestant
Reformation
Begins

Because this book is the story of Luther's life and because Luther's work was centered in Germany, we have said little about what was going on in the rest of Europe. All over Europe discontent with the Roman Church and rebellion against the Pope were causing trouble, so that what Luther did was only part of what was happening. In the German portion of Switzerland Ulrich Zwingli, who was less than a year younger than Luther, was saying in his own way much of what Luther was saying and was starting reforms in the churches there. In the French portion of Switzerland John Calvin, who was sixteen years younger than Luther, came later and founded the churches which we now know as Presbyterian or Reformed. In France there was a strong movement against the Roman Church, which was later put down by force. In many countries there were groups of people, called Anabaptists, whose ideas of reforming the Church went to such extremes that men like Luther and Zwingli thought them wild and outrageous. In England King Henry VIII was having all sorts of trouble with the Pope, but he was still trying to keep the Roman Church's ideas and practices undisturbed. When Henry first read one of Luther's books, he was furious. He wrote an answer to the book in which he said, "What pest so pernicious as Luther has ever attacked the flock of Christ? What a wolf of hell he is! What a limb of Satan!" The Pope was so pleased with Henry that he gave him the title "Defender of the Faith," but a few years later the English church broke completely away from Rome and became the Church of Eng-

The peasants burned castles and monasteries

land. And in northern Europe, in Denmark, Sweden and Norway, Luther's ideas were spreading fast. So what we now call the Protestant Reformation was going forward in various ways all over Europe.

Meanwhile Luther himself had his hands full of trouble in Germany, where the fight was growing hotter and hotter.

One of the worst things that ever happened to Luther was the Peasants' War. The peasants were the poor people, especially the farmers, who suffered all sorts of unjust oppression. They wanted almost everything changed, not only in the Church but in the way they were treated in everyday life. At first Luther sympathized with them and urged the princes to heed their demands. When, however, the princes refused and began trying to put them down by tough means, the peasants grew more and more angry until at last they broke loose in a wild war. They burned castles and monasteries, and murdered those who opposed them. In one German principality alone, Franconia, they burned 270 castles and 52 monasteries and nunneries. Luther was thoroughly dismayed and frightened. "They rob and rage and act like mad dogs," he said. Moreover, his enemies were saying that Luther started it all, that his ideas had upset everybody, and that he was to blame. So Luther saw no way out except to urge the princes to crush the rebellion by force. He wrote a dreadful tract, urging everyone to attack the riotous peasants, in which he said, "Therefore, let everyone who can do it smite, slay and stab, secretly or openly, remembering that nothing can be more poisonous, hurtful or devilish than a rebel. It is just as when one must kill a mad dog; if you don't strike him, he will strike you and the whole land with you."

Writing *that* was one of the worst things Luther ever did. It has always been held against him. When, however, the princes did "smite, slay and stab," crushing the peasants without mercy, Luther changed his tune. He had said at first that there were no devils left in hell, because they all had come out to enter the peasants. Now he said that the devils, instead of returning to hell, had entered the victorious princes. He condemned their cruelty toward the beaten peasants and did his best to end the outrageous struggle.

This Peasants' War lost Luther many friends. Some of the peasants turned against him, and some of the German rulers, blaming him for the whole wretched affair, swung to the Roman Catholic side. Perhaps worst of all was the effect on Luther himself. Always after that he distrusted the common people's ability to handle public affairs, and relied more and more on the German ruling classes to get what he wanted done.

This does not mean that he did not keep on making his strong appeal to the common people. He did. He was one of them. He understood what they were thinking and he spoke their language. We must not think of Roman Catholicism in Luther's day as being merely a matter of indulgences, pilgrimages, sacred relics and all that kind of thing. Multitudes of plain folk in Germany were not simply Roman Catholics in these outward matters; they were genuine Christians in their lives. They believed in God and in Jesus Christ, they found strength in prayer, they read their

Bibles, and they tried to live upright and useful lives. When Luther talked about this vital kind of Christianity—faith in Christ that changed men's characters—they knew what he meant. And when he said that *this* was what really mattered in Christianity and that many of the outward practices on which the Pope insisted were either unnecessary or positively false and dangerous, many of them agreed with him. They agreed not simply because they disliked the Pope for one reason or another, but because they felt in their hearts that they could be genuine Christians without the Pope. So Luther's strong support came not so much from priests and official leaders of the Church as from plain people. One Lutheran pamphlet of the time said that all over Germany were housewives, maids, students, handworkers, tailors, shoemakers and bakers, as well as nobles and princes, "who know more about the Bible than all the schools of Paris and Cologne and all the papists in the world."

Despite all Luther's troubles, therefore—like the Peasants' War—his popular support continued to grow. But how to change the churches and so put a stop to the sale of indulgences, the veneration of sacred relics, the use of sacred statues, prayers to the saints and many other practices which Luther thought wrong—*that* was the problem. Who was to take charge and see that the changes were made in good order? The only answer seemed to be that the prince must take charge. In Saxony this certainly seemed to be the answer. There Frederick, the ruler, was friendly to Luther, and when he died his brother John, who succeeded him, was even more enthusiastic about Luther's reforms. So Luther turned to the prince, who appointed a commission, and under the direction of the prince the churches of Saxony were gradually reformed until Luther's ideas were put into practice.

Anyone can see what the result was bound to be if this sort of thing went on all over Germany. The result would not be anything like what we Americans stand for—the separation of church and state. The result would be that the church would come under the control of the state, and that is exactly what happened. If in any province of Germany the prince was a Roman Catholic, the churches remained Roman Catholic. If in any province the prince was a Lutheran, the churches became Lutheran. One can easily imagine the unhappy situation of Roman Catholics who happened to live under Lutheran princes, and of Lutherans who happened to live under Roman Catholic princes. If they wanted churches which they could conscientiously worship in, they had to move their homes to another province.

At that time there seemed to be no other way of handling the situation, but Luther was disturbed by it. It gave the princes too much control over the religious life of their subjects. Often the Lutheran princes dealt hardly with their Roman Catholic citizens, and Catholic princes made life miserable for their Lutheran citizens. Luther did not for a moment think that any man ought to accept his religion because a prince told him to do so. "Over the soul," he said, "God can and will let no one rule except himself alone." Luther really believed in individual religious liberty. In those days when religious persecution was almost universally practiced both by Protestants and Roman Catholics, and when in country after country thousands of so-called heretics, who did not agree with the religion which happened to be in power, were burned at the stake, Luther stood out against such persecution. He said that he was "terrified" by the cruel history of it. "I cannot admit," he wrote, "that false teachers are to be put to death. It is enough to banish them." As for an individual who was being forced by a prince to go against his conscience, that man, said Luther, must resist the prince. Jesus told us, wrote Luther, that for God's sake we are to leave father and mother; surely, then, for God's sake we must forsake a prince.

Nevertheless, in the confusion of those days, there seemed to be no other way to arrange matters peaceably except by letting each German ruler determine the religion of his own province. Of course, the Roman Catholics also hated this arrangement. It meant that they were permitting a large part of Germany, under Lutheran princes, to accept and put into practice Lutheran ideas. But they could not find another way of handling the matter, any more than the Lutherans could. So the Second Diet of Speyer in 1529, where the Catholics had a majority, accepted the arrangement, but they saved their faces by a very disturbing provision. In Lutheran lands, the Diet said, the Catholics must have religious liberty, but in Catholic lands the same liberty would not be extended to Lutherans. Against this, and some other anti-Lutheran decisions of the Diet, the followers of Luther made a vehement protest. They said that "they must protest and testify publicly before God that they could consent to nothing contrary to his Word." That is where the name "Protestant" came from. It never had been used before. After that it became more and more the name commonly given not only to Lutherans but to all Christians in western Europe who had broken away from the Roman Church.

While the arrangement that we have described was a compromise which satisfied no one, it did open the door for Luther to help organize his new kind of church in all the parts of Germany where Lutheran princes ruled. That was his major task for the rest of his life. He settled down in Wittenberg and went on with his teaching in the university, but day and night he was concerned about all the German churches that had come under the influence of his ideas. He preached about what should be done, visited churches far and wide, and from the printing press scores of pamphlets which he wrote poured forth to be distributed to his followers. Little by little the way public worship was conducted was changed. Instead of Latin, which Roman Catholics used and which the plain people did not understand, the German language was used. The sermon was made more important than it ever had been before. A German Bible lay on every pulpit and the people had copies of the Bible in their pews. Instead of the Roman Catholic Mass, what we call the Lord's Supper was substituted. And all sorts of old practices such as the sale of indulgences, the veneration of sacred relics, pilgrimages, prayers to the saints and all the schemes for getting souls out of purgatory were stopped. Protestantism was really getting under way.

One of the most popular changes which Luther introduced was congregational singing in the churches. Here Luther's love of music came to the front again. In the Roman service singing was almost altogether confined to the priest and the choir. Luther published a hymn book so that all the people could sing. In that first hymn book there were only twenty-three hymns, of all of which Luther himself was the author. Germans have always loved singing and now in the churches they made the most of it. One priest who hated Luther said that "the hymns of Luther killed more souls than his sermons." To this day one of the most rousing hymns that we sing is Luther's masterpiece:

A mighty fortress is our God,
A bulwark never failing.

To be sure, while all these changes were going forward, many serious people felt that it was a great tragedy for Christians to be split apart into separate and hostile churches. Christians ought to be united and stand together against the evil in the world. Surely, these serious people thought, there must be some way of healing the divisions and keeping Christians together in one Church. Not only were Protestants organized against Catholics, but the Protestants themselves were divided. So one attempt after another was made to stop the division of the Church and to bring all Christians together again.

Once Luther and Zwingli held a conference to see if the Zwinglians in Switzerland and the Lutherans in Germany could unite. They almost succeeded but not quite. There were differences between them about what the Lord's Supper meant and they parted without agreement. So at the very beginning Protestantism began splitting up into separate churches, until in the United States today there are some two hundred and fifty different kinds of Protestants.

Some of these serious people, who were distressed to see the Church of Christ broken into separate pieces, hoped that even Roman Catholics and Protestants might heal their differences and get together again. Gentle-spirited Philipp Melanchthon was one of these, and in 1530 at the Diet of Augsburg, where the Emperor was present, a final attempt was made to find a way to agreement and unity. Luther was interested in this too, but because he was an outlaw in the Emperor's eyes he could not attend the meeting of the Diet. He was left at Coburg, just inside Saxony where he was safe, about a hundred and thirty miles from Augsburg. There he stayed for six months, watching from a distance Melanchthon's endeavors to get the Roman Catholics and Protestants to agree. Still in existence are a hundred and twenty-five letters which Luther wrote from Coburg to his friends in Augsburg.

Melanchthon did his best. He prepared a statement —the Confession of Augsburg—that emphasized all the matters on which Catholics and Protestants agreed and that left out or toned down all the matters on which they disagreed. The Catholics were surprised and pleased at this, and they put the pressure on, trying to persuade the Lutherans to surrender one point after another. It did not work. The Protestants dug in their heels and would not surrender. Certainly

Luther would give in no more. At last he wrote from Coburg:

"I am almost bursting with wrath and indignation. I beg you will abruptly break off negotiations with them and return home. They have the Confession, they have the gospel. If they will, let them accept it. If they will not, let them go where they belong. If war comes, come it will; we have prayed and done enough."

So this final attempt to heal the breach between Roman Catholics and Protestants failed, and four hundred years ago the situation was created which we face yet, with the two kinds of Christian churches sharply divided. As for Germany, Luther went back to his life-work there—trying to make the Lutheran churches as strong and as Christian as he could.

10

Luther
Gets a
Home

L UTHER had never in-
tended to marry. When he became a monk he took
a solemn vow that he never would marry. The more
he thought about the matter, however, the more sure
he was that for priests at any rate, even if not for
monks, marriage was wise and right. One of the first
changes that took place when Luther's ideas were put
into practice was that priests began to get married.
Luther was an exile in Wartburg Castle when this
began and he approved of it. He thought that a priest

would be a better priest if he had a wife and children and a good home. Hearing about his friend Carlstadt's wedding, Luther wrote, "I am very pleased over Carlstadt's marriage. I know the girl."

At first, however, he was shocked at the idea that a *monk* should marry. He remembered the solemn oath he had sworn when he entered the monastery— never to take a wife. When at Wartburg Castle he first heard that monks and nuns in Wittenberg were leaving their cloisters, renouncing their vows and marrying, he was dismayed. "Good heavens!" he wrote, "Will our Wittenbergers give wives to monks? They won't give one to me!"

As the years passed, however, Luther changed his opinion about the right of a monk to marry. He decided that the vow which a monk takes against marrying was wrong and that a wrong vow ought not to be kept. Certainly *that* was what hundreds of monks and nuns were thinking. They were leaving their cloisters in a steady stream and were setting up homes of their own. Luther sympathized with them and approved of their action, but he had no idea of getting married himself.

In a nunnery not far from Wittenberg, however, there was a girl who was going to make Luther change his mind. Her name was Katherine von Bora. Her mother had died when she was a little child and her father, marrying again, had put her in a nunnery when she was not more than nine or ten years old. There were only about forty in that convent, many of them young girls like herself, and Katherine grew up there, not knowing any other kind of life. So, when she was sixteen she took the vows of a nun and settled down to spend the rest of her life in the cloister.

That cloister, however, was too near Wittenberg not to feel the effect of all the changes that were taking place, and finally a group of the girls made up their minds that they wanted to have homes of their own and that they had a right to have them. They appealed to Luther to help them escape from the convent, and he arranged the matter with a tradesman who occasionally delivered barrels of supplies to the nuns. Twelve girls gathered in Katherine's room one night, climbed out of the window into the garden, and then climbed over the wall to the street. There the tradesman met them, hid them in the empty barrels and drove them to Wittenberg. Three of the girls had homes to go to, but nine of them became Luther's responsibility. They had taken nothing with them from the convent and they were in great need. A friend of Luther's wrote a letter about them in which he said, "I pity the creatures. They have neither shoes nor clothes. My dearest brother, I beg, if you can get something for them from the court, you will supply them with food and clothing. You must make haste, for they are in great poverty and anxiety, but very patient. I wonder indeed how they can be so brave and merry when in such distress and want."

One by one these young women were married or otherwise provided for—all except Katherine von Bora. Two years after her escape from the convent she was still a domestic servant in a Wittenberg household, and she was not happy about it. Her un-

happiness was all the worse because she had fallen
in love with a student at the university who had proposed marriage to her and had been accepted but
who, when he went home, had changed his mind
and married someone else. Luther did not know what
to do with Katherine. He found another man for her,
a certain Dr. Glatz, who wanted to marry her, but
she did not like him and refused. One day, probably
laughing when she said it, she told a visitor in Wittenberg, Dr. Amsdorf, that she would not marry Dr.
Glatz but that she was quite willing to marry either
Dr. Amsdorf or Dr. Luther.

When Luther heard this, so far as we can judge,
he at first took it as a joke, but then he began thinking seriously about it. One reason he had been giving
for not marrying was that he did not know how
much longer he could escape the Emperor's wrath
and if he was going to be killed within a year it was
no time to start a home. Now, however, he began to
change his mind. "I believe in marriage," he wrote,
"and I intend to get married before I die." Then on
a visit to his parents he faced his father's strong de-

sire. Old Hans Luther wanted grandchildren. He wanted Martin to have a wife and a home, and he told his son so in stout language. Well, Martin wanted a home too. So he began to think of Katherine as a possible wife. She was not physically very beautiful, but she had charm, strong character and great ability. Not long afterward Martin proposed to her and she accepted. As anyone can see, it was not a wild, romantic love affair, but just the same it came out beautifully. Martin was forty-two years old and Katherine was twenty-six when they were married, and together they founded a loyal and happy home, concerning which years later Luther said, "It has turned out well, God be thanked! For I have a pious and true wife, on whom her husband's heart can rely."

Certainly Luther needed a wife. He may have been exaggerating a little when he said that in his bachelor days he used to leave his bed unmade for a year at a time, but he had been, to say the least, dreadfully careless about matters like that. Then Katherine took over. She was a forceful, energetic young woman and an excellent manager. Luther could do as he pleased about reforming the Church, but when it came to running the household Katherine took charge.

Like everybody in that generation, Luther had very old-fashioned ideas about family life. He thought the man was the head of the household and the wife's business was humbly to obey him. At first he seems to have been surprised at what had happened to him when he married Katherine. She was not by any means always obedient—not when it came to taking care of him and seeing to it that his home was well managed. "If I were to marry again," he once exploded, "I would carve me an obedient wife out of stone, for I doubt whether any wives are obedient." One suspects, therefore, that at the start Martin and Katherine had the usual difficulties learning to live together. He had a stormy temper and she had a spirited tongue. "There is a lot to get used to in the first year of marriage," Luther once said. In the end, however, Katherine held her ground and Luther loved her for it. He had every reason to. One wonders how he ever would have got through the last twenty years of his life without her. Far from expecting her to take his word for everything, he used to call her "my lord Katie."

In Wittenberg Luther had lived in a monastery—a building large enough to accommodate forty monks. Now, however, all the monks had left, and the prince gave the building to Luther. So Katherine had a large establishment to care for, and she certainly took good care of it. Luther was in debt when he married, and "lord Katie" soon got him out of that. He had been very careless about money, and was so generous that he gave away anything he possessed whenever he felt like it. Katie stopped that. In one letter which Luther wrote to a friend, telling him that he was sending him a vase for a wedding present, he added a postscript saying that Katie had hidden the vase and so he couldn't send it.

Moreover, she put Luther to work in the garden and he loved it. There they grew lettuce, cabbage, peas, beans, melons and cucumbers. Later they bought a farm outside of Wittenberg and Katherine managed that and made a great success of it. In one letter of Luther's which has come down to us he says, "My lord Katie greets you. She plants our fields; she pastures and sells cows, etc. In between she has started to read the Bible. I have promised her fifty gulden if she finishes by Easter. She is hard at it, and is at the end of the fifth book of Moses."

Not content with all this, Katherine made good use of the extra rooms in the old monastery by taking in student boarders, so that her household commonly numbered as many as twenty-five people whom she housed and fed. Luther loved that too. He always enjoyed having a social group around him. One reason why we know so much about the everyday, human side of Luther and about the way he thought and talked, is that the students soon began taking notes of what he said at the dinner table. They jotted down his remarks on almost every imaginable subject and, after his death, they gathered these remarks together—6,596 of them—and published them. Reading them now, one can fairly see Luther in his informal hours, with his jovial good nature, his rough humor, his boisterous laughter and, underneath all, his sturdy courage and conscientiousness.

Martin and Katie had six children, and Martin loved that too. When the first child was born Luther wrote to a friend, "My dear Katie brought into the world yesterday by God's grace, at two o'clock, a little son, Hans Luther. I must stop. Sick Katie is calling me." As was always done in those days, they bound the new-born baby all up in swaddling clothes. And as Luther looked at him he said, "Kick, little fellow. That's what the Pope did to me, but I got loose." Luther was a devoted father. To be sure, he had his troublesome times trying to bring up six children. Once he laughingly remarked, "Christ said we must become as little children. Dear God, this is too much. Have we got to become such idiots?" That, however, was only a passing jest. Luther loved children. Some Protestants—we call them "Puritans" now—were rather afraid of fun and were very strict and stern. Luther was not like that at all. He wanted children to enjoy themselves and he encouraged them to dance, play games, put on theatrical shows and sing.

So Luther had a home of his own, and for twenty years it was the sustaining background of his life.

In his later years Luther was not well. Most men would have quit and gone to bed, but Luther never stopped his work for the reformation of the Church till the very end. Once, toward the close of his life, he described himself as "old, decrepit, lazy, worn out, cold, and now one-eyed," but still he kept on. When he died he was on a journey, trying to patch up a quarrel between two Lutheran nobles, and death caught up with him in Eisleben—the very town where more than sixty-two years earlier he had been born.

Luther was one of the strongest characters in history. He must have had a dreadful struggle at times controlling himself, for he was so high-powered that when he was in a good mood he was naturally boisterous and when he was angry he was furious. He did not by any means always succeed in controlling himself. Once in a while, when he was all upset, he would write a letter which he ought never to have written.

Once one of his students asked him why he was so violent and he answered, "A twig can be cut with a bread knife, but an oak calls for an ax." That is the way he thought of himself—as an ax whose business it was to cut down a tough oak. So he slugged away at it and, despite his mistakes, he made one of the greatest contributions any man ever made to our modern world. Underneath all these stormy qualities in Luther, however, he was a modest man full of good nature and kindliness. Before he died all northern Europe was strongly under his influence, and the churches there were calling themselves by his name. He did not like that. He wrote a protest against it, in which he said:

> "I pray you leave my name alone and call yourselves not 'Lutherans' but 'Christians.' Who is Luther? My teaching is not mine. I have not been crucified for anyone. . . . How then does it befit me, a miserable bag of dust and ashes, to give my name to the children of Christ? Cease, my dear friends, to cling to these party names and distinctions; away with them all; let us call ourselves

only 'Christians' after Him from whom our teaching comes!"

That was Luther at his best, and we are all unpayably indebted to him.

Appendix

WHEN IT HAPPENED

1483 November 10	Martin Luther born in Eisleben.
1484 Summer	Family moved to Mansfield.
1497 Easter	Luther went to school in Magdeburg.
1498–1501	Luther at school in Eisenach.
1501 May	Luther entered University of Erfurt.
1502 September 29	Luther received his Bachelor's degree.
1505 January 7	Luther received his Master's degree.
1505 July 17	Luther became a monk.
1510 November	Luther's trip to Rome.
1511 April	Luther became professor at University of Wittenberg.
1512 October 19	Luther received his Doctor's degree.

1517 October 31	Luther nailed his ninety-five theses to church door.
1518 August 7	The Pope summoned Luther to Rome.
1518 October 12–14	Luther's interview with Cajetan.
1519 January 4–6	Luther's interview with von Miltitz.
1519 July	The Leipzig debate.
1520 June 15	The Pope gave Luther sixty days to submit.
1520 December 10	Luther burned the Pope's bull.
1521 April 16	Luther in Worms.
1521 May 4	Luther in exile in Wartburg Castle.
1522 March	Luther returned to Wittenberg.
1522 September	Luther's German New Testament published.
1525 March to June	The Peasants' War.
1525 June 13	Luther's betrothal to Katherine von Bora.
1529 April 19	The "protest" at the Diet of Speyer.
1530 April to June	The Diet of Augsburg.
1546 February 18	Luther's death in Eisleben.

INDEX

A mighty fortress" (hymn), 156
Address to the German Nobility, 106
Albert, Prince, 59–60, 63
Aleander, Cardinal, 107–10
Alexander VI, Pope, 43
Amsdorf, Dr., 167
Anabaptists, 144
Anne, Saint, 10, 28
Astronomy, 14
Augsburg, Diet of, 158, 180
Augsburg conference, 84–86
Augsburg Confession, 158–59
Augustine, Saint, books, 52
Augustinian monastery, Erfurt, 28–30, 33–43
Augustinian monastery, Wittenberg, 43–44
Augustinian monks, 74–75
"Away in a manger" (hymn), 11

B *abylonian Captivity of the Church*, 106
Begging, 36–37
Bible (The), 51–53, 95–97, 131, 150
Bible translations, 128–29
Black Bear Inn, 132
Bohemia, 105
Bora, Katherine von, 165–72, 180
Bull denouncing Luther, 98–99, 103, 104, 107–09, 113, 180

C ajetan, Cardinal, 84–86, 88, 180
Calvin, John, 144
Carlstadt, Andreas, 91–92, 138, 164
Catholic Encyclopedia, 57
Charles V, Emperor, 5–6, 104, 107–15
Children:
    Luther's love for, 172–73
    poverty, 8
    scaring, 12
    whipping, 8–9
Christ, 12, 52, 53, 55, 56
Christianity, 135, 150, 157, 173

Church and state, separation of, 151–52
Church councils, 95–98, 105, 113
Coburg, Germany, 158–59
Columbus, 13–14
Confession, 44–45, 52, 55
Congregational singing, 156
Conscience, 6, 114, 153
Constance church council, 105
Copernicus, 14–15
Corpus Juris, 26
Cotta, Frau (foster mother), 21, 23
Crusades, 56

D emons, 13
Denmark, 147
Devil(s), 13, 40, 76, 109–10, 125, 148
Devil and ink pot story, 125
Dominican monks, 74, 78
Dürer, Albrecht, 116

E arth, 14
Eck, John, 91–92, 96–98, 104, 105
Eisenach, Germany, 20–21, 23–24, 116, 179
Eisleben, Germany, 7, 173, 179, 180
England, 144–45
Erasmus, 58
Erfurt, Germany, 24–26, 28, 30, 37, 51–52, 179
Ex cathedra pronouncements, 78

F airies, 13
Family life, 169
Feudalism, 70
France, 144
Franconia (principality), 147
Frankfort-on-the-Oder, University, 75
Frederick, Elector of Saxony, 44, 58–59, 78–79, 83–84, 86, 107–09, 119, 151
Freedom of the Christian Man, 107

family life, 169
farm, 170–71
fasting, 37, 51
fears, 27, 46, 53, 125
flogging, 38, 51
foster mother, 21
humor, 172
hymn for children, 10–11
kidnaping of, 116, 119
language, 23, 112
laughter, 172
letters, 158–59, 170, 173
lute playing, 25–26
manners, 22–23
marriage, 26–27, 163–69
mass, first, 38–39
mistakes, 173
moderation, 38
monastery, entry into, 28–30, 179
music, 10–11, 25–26, 156
obedience, 36
parents, 7–9, 12, 19
personal qualities, 89
personality, 21, 24–25, 135
prayer periods, 37–38
preaching, 46, 49–50
priest, consecrated as, 38–39
punishments, 12
rebirth, 53
recantation, 108
religion, 11, 15, 26, 54–55
remarks, 171–72
resentfulness, 9
self-denials, 38
self-description, 76
self-punishments, 38, 46
sensitivity, 8, 12
sermons, 50, 53, 59, 136, 156
singing, 21, 25
sleep, 37
soul, 33–34, 37, 44, 51, 53, 89
teaching, 51–53
temper, 169
tough side, 22–23
trial, 5–6, 78–79
violence, 173
youth, 5–15
Luther, Mrs. Martin, 165–72
Luther family:
children, 9–10
manners, 21–22
religion, 9–10
Lutheran (name), 173–74
Lutheran Churches, 157, 159

Magdeburg, Germany, 20–21, 179
Mansfield, Germany, 7, 12–14, 19, 27, 179
Marriage, 126–27, 163–69
Mass(es), 42–43, 127, 136
Maximilian, Emperor, 104
Melanchthon, Philipp, 76–77, 126, 131, 134, 157–58
Mendicants, 36–37
Miltitz, Carl von, 86–91, 180
Mines, miners, 10, 13
Mohre, Germany, 7
Monastery life, rules of, 36–38
Monks, 163–67, 179
Music, 26

New Testament, 128, 180
Ninety-Five Theses, 64, 67–69, 74, 91, 180
Norway, 147
Nurnberg assembly, 137

Old Testament, 128–29
Orlamunde, Germany, 138

Parents, honor for, 39–40, 153
Paul, Saint, 52
Peartree episode, 46
Peasants' revolts, 114–15
Peasants' War, 147–49, 180
Penance, acts of, 53, 55
Pilgrimages, 52–53, 55, 57
Plague (epidemic), 30
Pope (The):
Bible, 96
bull against Luther, 98–99, 103, 104, 107–09, 113, 180
differing with, 90
foreign sovereign, regarded as, 72–73
indulgences, 56–60, 68–70, 77–78, 83–88, 92, 95
mistakes, 95–97
purgatory, 69
rebellion against, 143
Poverty, 7–8
Presbyterian Church, 144
Prierias, Sylvester, 78–79
Priests, 42–43, 126, 131, 163–64
Printing, invention of, 51

LANDMARK BOOKS

WORLD LANDMARK BOOKS